Runway Uncovered
The Making of a Fashion Show

Runway Uncovered

The Making of a Fashion Show

Estel Vilaseca

Runway Uncovered. The Making of a Fashion Show
Editorial project: **maomao** publications

Editorial Coordinator: Anja Llorella Oriol
Editor: Estel Vilaseca
Texts: Estel Vilaseca
Editorial Assistant: Borja Rodríguez
Translation: Cillero & de Motta
Layout concept: Estel Vilaseca
Art Director: Emma Termes Parera
Layout: Maira Purman
Cover design: Emma Termes Parera
Cover picture: Armani Privé haute couture spring 2009
runway. © Photography by David Ramos

Copyright @ 2010 English edition by Promopress

PROMOPRESS is a brand of:
PROMOTORA DE PRENSA INTERNACIONAL SA
Ausias March, 124
08013 Barcelona, Spain
T: + 34 932 451 464
F: + 34 932 654 883
E-mail: info@promopress.es
www.promopress.info

First published in English: 2010
ISBN 978-84-92810-06-2
Printed in Spain

The basic qualities

What is a runway show? To define means to describe the basic qualities of something and we must add many specifications to a definition to explain it properly. A collection of clothes, a group of models, a stage and an audience are the main ingredients of this short performance, which is organized to present the designer's latest collection. A marketing tool, a means of communication or activity through which the leitmotiv of a collection must be correctly conveyed, the runway show has an open and ever-changing format. The lights go off and there is complete silence on the runway. Backstage, everyone is running around. The designer quickly makes the final touches to the first outfit. The model who opens the show receives the signal from the runway show director and walks out onto the stage. The show begins.

Valentino haute couture spring 2009. The Sorbonne, Paris. © Photography by David Ramos.

Definition

The runway show is a means through which the designer can convey their ideas, publicize the label, get coverage in the media and gain loyalty from the public.[1] Didier Grumbach, president of the Fédération Française de la Couture has the following opinion: "There is no regulation forcing designers to put on a public runway show, but they want to be seen and there is nothing like a runway show to exhibit their art. It's a way of expressing their ideas, it's a resource".[2]

Once the designer has come up with and made the collection, the main priority is to get it out there, and the runway is the ideal way to communicate this, as it is one of the best ways to really see the fall and the proportions of the garments on the models while they are moving. "In Yohji Yamamoto's work, concepts such as the nature of change and remodeling are explored, which can be clear-

ly appreciated when his fluid and architectural garments are present on a moving runway", Claire Wilcox explains.[3]

The press and buyers are their main audience as well as regular clients and friends. The buyers will confirm their decision to buy, which they have made weeks before the show, and they may make another order, while the press from newspapers and specialist magazines will report on the collection. They will also keep an eye out for certain looks that they can use for future editions.[4]

In order to do so, you only need a select few to let the splendor of the product shine through, one place to do it and one public.[5] From this moment onwards, the variety of formats is numerous and countless.

The different runway shows organized around the world are held twice a year —January-February and September-October— in annual calendar taking into account

LEFT Joe Edney and Matvey Lykov model the Y-3 spring-summer 2008 collection, by Yohji Yamamoto and Adidas, in the Chelsea neighborhood in New York. © Photography by Mark Reay. **TOP** Details of the fall-winter 2009 collection by Sophia Kokosalaki in Paris. © Photography by Gerard Estadella.

RIGHT Closure of the haute couture spring 2009 collection by Christian Lacroix, held in The Pompidou Center, Paris. © Photography by David Ramos.

the design, production, distribution and sale of the collections, which have already been designed the previous year. In fall, the haute couture and prêt-à-porter collections of the spring-summer collection of the following year are presented and in spring the fall-winter collections. New York, London, Milan and Paris, traditionally, are the fashion weeks with most prestige and with the most press coverage, but recently capitals such as Copenhagen, Berlin and Sydney are gaining ground, particularly in more independent publications. For some fashion publishing houses, following the calendar is a complicated task, and for this reason the choice of the suitable place, day and location for the runway show should be studied carefully.

One show after another is what builds a designer's image and makes them stand out to the public, positioning them in the market.[6] Buyers prefer not to take risks, and normally wait for a few seasons before buying a new designer's collection as they want to check that the house will produce a top-quality collection and can professionally cope with large orders.[7]

A runway show is an ideal promotional tool, but it is also very expensive and does not always involve a direct economic compensation. Only if there is an increase in orders on account of positive reports from their collection will they recoup part of the investment. Thus, it is vital not to get carried away and choose a runway show format suited to the philosophy of the label and plan all details with the utmost care and professionalism. If the content of the collection is not up to standard, with little impact, and the show is not professional, this can damage the designer's credibility and their pocket.

The fashion presentations are more and more diverse, adapting new formats and formulas, sometimes this is down to economic grounds and on other occasions it is more to do with the philosophy of the actual label. One of the first decisions to be made is to select and suitably present the collection.

For newcomers, the majority of experts advise a simpler format than a runway show, such as a short and concise presentation, in which the garments are the main stars, leaving the flamboyancy for when the label is more established and when there is a larger budget available to deliver a top quality show. In a short space of time, a designer puts his/her career on the line by putting their work out for the public vote: "The ready-to-wear runway shows make or break a designer's career".[8] In this sense, new technologies have become an ally for

designers who have a small budget but good ideas.

The objectives of a runway show
In a runway show there are several and multiple objectives:

To PRESENT NEW COLLECTIONS. In order to do so, the collection must be presented in an attractive and suggestive way in line with the idea and the style that the designer wishes to convey.
The prior press release and press dossier are two necessary complements so that reporters are aware of who the garments are aimed at and what they want to convey with them. Apart from presenting their garments,

designers are offering implicit information about the label: sophistication, alternative, conceptual, artistic or Bohemian.

To ATTRACT MEDIA ATTENTION. Seduction captures the attention of the press so that the collection becomes an object of desire.[9] Novelty, innovation and splendor are normally the most exploited resources.
Press photos and reporters working on the runway shows exemplify the commercial reality that exists behind the show, a reality that can be better seen at the end of the runway and among the audience even more so than on the actual runway show itself, where

TOP In the Bless runway show, the models are friends and customers of the label. In the image, the presentation of the 36th collection entitled Nothingneath was held in a typical Parisian hotel in Le Marais neighborhood. The models dressed in the new collection garments posed in a real-life contemporary background, in the narrow staircase of the building, allowing guests to establish closer contact with them. © Photography by Heinz Peter Knes, courtesy of Bless. **RIGHT** The models Behati Prinsloo, Julia Stegner and Kinga Rajzak closed the Airbone fall-winter 2007 runway show collection by Hussein Chalayan with a production that is very close to an artistic performance. © Photography by Chris Moore, courtesy of Hussein Chalayan.

the extravagant productions are calculated to hide this very commercial reality.[10]

To BE REMEMBERED. Fashion editors watch a large number of runway shows during fashion week: if something has managed to grab their attention, what is important is to be remembered and remain in their retina so that when they write up articles they decide to talk about the designs they have seen. A faultless production, a well-prepared press note and a combination of carefully-made garments are key elements to achieve a compact outfit regardless of whether or not the format is utterly spec-tacular and theatrical or simple and minimalist as, in the end, the garments are what matters.

To SUPPORT THE DECISION TO BUY. In a runway show, an important part of the public are buyers and possible buyers. For those who are already buyers, it is a good way to reaffirm their decision to buy and graciously show their loyalty. For future buyers, the runway show is an effective way to convince them.

To GENERATE EXPECTATION. If through their runway show designers manage to attract the attention of the press and buyers, they will see their names splashed across fashion magazines, and when they present their next collection many will want to attend. Their work must be consistent before, during and after the runway show.

Emotion and seduction

Designers, reporters, art directors and producers often mention the use of seduction and emotion as one of the best resources to achieve some of the objectives mentioned here. Designer Miuccia Prada explains: "Once I asked Louise Bourgeois why people are so interested in fashion, and she said: 'It's about seduction.'"[11] Expose yourself, model on the runway, capture

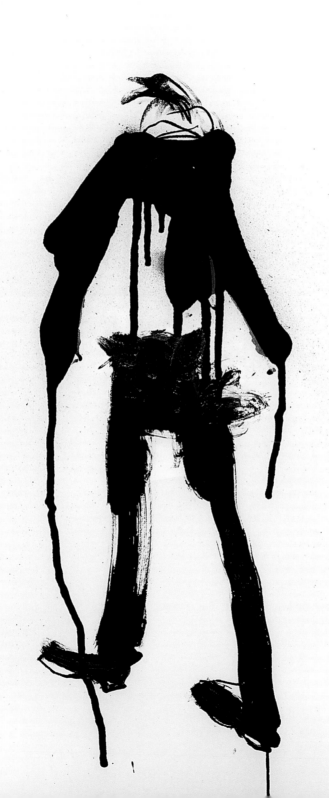

and attract attention. Look, look again, feel intoxicated and look one last again, runway shows use seduction wisely.

The reporter Jess Cartner-Morley defines the designer Dries van Noten's shows as "occasions of grandeur and emotion,"[12] to which the designer responds: "I put my soul into the shows." Following on with the use of proper adjectives from the most romantic literature, the reporter Susannah Frankel explains why the best runway shows are in Paris: "Only in Paris does fashion really make the heart beat faster. Coming to the end of an arduous international month-long season, the French ready-to-wear collections never fail to inspire and even move an audience to tears."[13]

Thierry Dreyfus, the lighting designer, talks about the importance of provoking emotion and achieving a real and emotional connection between the designer's ideas and the public, apart

from just trying to sell more garments, something that according to him is difficult and rare to achieve. The rest is down to pure and meaningless marketing.

The runway show director Alexandre de Betak adds: "With live shows you can manipulate people's emotions directly. [...] I calculate every quarter of a second. [...] Fashion shows have become more spectacular not for the show itself, but to become more TV-genic."[14]

The production

A runway show is a production that requires the participation of different teams and demands painstaking planning. For this reason, a detailed production plan is a must, and work must begin months before the big day.

Due to the large quantity of work and effort involved, on may occasions, designers do not produce the shows themselves, at least not fully, and they use production companies to take charge of the stage setting, the sound, the lighting, as well as the selection of models, the fittings, establishing the order of appearance, matching accessories, and coordinating stylists, hairdressers and make-up artists, and they also take charge of security, catering and arranging the seating.[15]

The type of collaboration between the designer and the production company changes depending on the designer. Some designers take part in the entire production process alongside the production company and their employees and offer precise and detailed information to each of the team members. On the other hand, others prefer to outline a few basic guidelines and place their trust in the hired team. Production companies such as Eyesight, Villa Eugénie and Bureau Betak have become indispensable for many designers as they have teams capable of making the most impossible demands a reality. Holographic apparitions of famous models, unusual locations, exquisite lighting and surreal hairstyles are a few eccentricities only for companies with the more generous budgets.

For those with discreet funds, the label manages the production itself; sometimes the press office lends a hand by coordinating the different teams and preparing the different schedules and chronograms.

The budget

A runway show is a large-scale ephemeral communication tool. In spite of its short duration (gen-

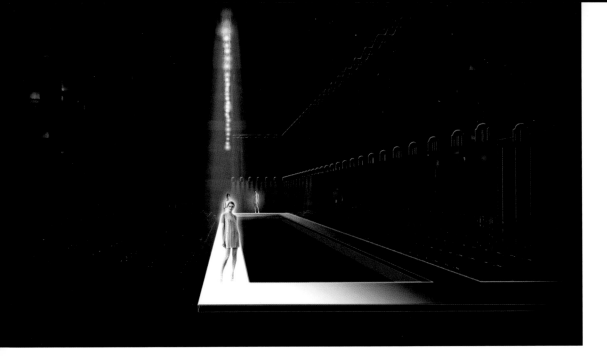

erally no longer than twenty minutes), there is a large investment of time and money in its design and development. According to recent market figures, a runway show for an independent designer costs a minimum of 30,000 euros; it costs between 150,000 to 300,000 euros to produce a show for a label that is a regular in the main fashion shows and up to 850,000 to finance an haute couture superproduction in Paris.[16] According to the experts, depending on the amount invested, if the show is carried out appropriately, designers can generate between ten and one hundred times the cost of the show in free publicity, photos in magazines, newspapers and blogs, television coverage, etc.[17]

However, for newcomers, there are some fashion weeks that of-fer suitable frameworks so that they are able to present their first collection with as little economic impact as possible for the designers through sponsorship. Likewise, others try to find cosmetic, hairdresser or drinks sponsors. It is necessary to assess the budget prior to everything else in order to maximize the benefits of time and effort for the entire team.

From ideas to magazines

From the initial concept to its appearance in specialized media and press, the runway show has several different stages and agents to produce it.

Once the collection is ready and the designer and the team are making the pieces that will be showed, it is important to think about how to present them with regards to the budget and the la-

LEFT Sketch with the design of the spring-summer 2009 runway show by Isaac Mizrahi done by interior designer Michael Brown, who on this occasion collaborated with the lighting designer Michael Chybowski. RIGHT It is interesting to check the fidelity in the creation of the idea and how the majority of the details are not down to chance but they have been worked on weeks ahead. © Photography by Michael Brown

bel's positioning in the world of fashion. If the designer chooses to present the collection within the framework of fashion week, they will be restricted to a certain location. On other occasions, if the dates coincide with the fashion week of the designer's native country, they can choose to present it in a surprising location.

It is important that behind the runway show there is a concept that unifies the collection as a compact and coherent ensemble. Production, models, lighting, music, style, makeup and hairstyles must respond to this general idea, without any of these elements standing out over the others. Finding a balance is something that requires effort and experience. To conceive an idea, the designer must rely on the support of an art director, who may be a free-lancer or a member of a runway show production company team. Together they define the production and the guidelines to follow. If the designer is clear on the type of show, choosing the right professionals to produce and letting them know what is expected of each of them will be a lot easier. Along with the stage designer, the art director will decide the production process. Theatrical, minimalist or conceptual, everything depends on the idea that they have in mind. The art director will be in charge of the relevant sketches and create them with the team. The lighting designer is another essential figure in the success of a good runway show. A specific ambience will be created with proper lighting, models will have a certain complexion and the audience attention will be focused on the details highlighted by the lighting. No runway show is complete without an accompanying sound track. A skilled sound artist will search out and mix the musical themes that best adapt to the selected concept. On some occasions, the designer invites a band to perform live, converting this piece into a fundamental added value to gain more press coverage.

Along with the stylist, the designer will coordinate all the outfits to convey a specific, legible message for all editors sitting in the front rows. A good combination of garments is essential so that the collection has a good name. Together they will decide on suitable hairstyles and makeup to go with the collection. The hair stylist and the makeup artist will offer several possible alternatives

LEFT Backstage, where models get their hair and makeup done and they change, must be extremely organized. Each model has his/her own area with clear instructions for all the outfits that they will wear on the runway. © Photography by Eric Oliveira. **RIGHT** In fifteen minutes a designer presents six months of work. A lot of effort must be made for the presentation to be flawless. In the image, Antonio Marras finalizes the last minute details before the Milan runway show begins. © Photography by Eric Oliveira.

until they find the right one that the models will sport on the day of the show. The casting director will decide who will model, and along with the stylist they will give each model the outfits that they will wear on the big day. The producer and the runway show manager create the choreography, the order of the show and the timing of the team.

The overall and coherent management of all these elements is essential to achieve an effective solution and ensure that the message that they want to convey is clear, not only for those at the show but also for the media coverage on the event.

After so much preparation, it is important that on the day of the runway show the specialized press and buyers who fit into the philosophy of the designer's label are present and that the designer does not disappoint them so as to achieve the maximum possible impact. The press office is in charge of putting together the guest list, sending out the invites, making the formal announcement, and deciding on the seating arrangement. The invitations to attend the runway or the press dossier and gifts designed exclusively for the occasion are vital communication elements. They help define the atmosphere and attract the correct public, as well as being unique elements that last long after the event is over.[18] They must be designed carefully.[19] Many designers rely on major communication studies to manufacture them, converting the invitations into authentic collectors' items.

On the day of the runway show, it only takes twenty minutes to exhibit six months of work.

The emotion, the live adrenaline and the space for small errors make up the DNA of this type of presentation. The day after the show, the press office must draw up a press note on the event and accompany it with photographs of the show, the backstage and the guests so that the press can use them as they wish. It is also important that, once the runway show has finished, and taking into account that it is already

out there in the public domain, the website should be updated straight away. Reporters, customers, future buyers and followers of the label who could not attend the show will more than likely watch it later online.

LEFT The Paris runway shows manage to attract the largest amount of well-known faces that in turn attract the press. The actress Dita Von Teese leaves the Dior runway show. © Photography by David Ramos. RIGHT The iconic Karl Lagerfeld talks to the media during the haute couture week in Paris. © Photography by David Ramos.

Henrik Vibsk

Designer
www.henrikvibskov.com

Henrik Vibskov is a desig
to do things his own way.
his menswear collections
his women's collections i
Denmark, where he is a re
always remaining loyal t
which separates the ortho
unusual. His multisensory
discipline runway shows
from the revival style and
the world of art; they are c
and have become his ha
skov is a self-made creato
to escape conventionality
still manages to fit his phil
the parameters of the syste

What is a runway show for Henrik Vibskov?

The sensation of a universe created with as many elements as possible for at least twenty minutes. Colors, structures and how people interact interests me and I like to communicate casually with them whether it is a thought, feeling or a situation. For example, I presented a runway show based on doing my laundry for the fall-winter 2009 collection.

Where do you find your ideas for your nonconformist presentations?

I draw inspiration from many sources. Simply, I have a specific life perspective that reflects in all of my work. Although it probably dawns on me when I am sitting in my garden in Copenhagen. The Solar Donkey Experiment runway show revolved around communication, and analogical communications were present both in the concept of the installation and in the presentation of the collection. The models were accompanied by donkeys: they represented the slowness, all that is analogical. It almost seemed as if we were trying to communicate with the rest of the world with a certain

"For future runway shows, more music, more people, more animals and more inspiration"

type of mobile mechanical installation.

How much preparation time do you need for a runway show?

It depends on the staging, but normally we start within two months. In The Big Wet Shiny Boobies presentation for the spring-summer 2007 collec-

tion, we made the boobies from three different molds with positive and negative forms and we had to do many trial runs. It was all very toxic . . .. But back to the question, the schedule changes so often that it is very difficult to plan ahead. In particular, because there are many phases that overlap.

Do you work with a production agency or prepare the runway show internally?

We prepare it ourselves. I have a team that I have worked with for years and they do a great job. There are about twenty of us. For example, deciding on the combination of garments that will appear on the runway involves a lot of people from my team; however, I also have a clear idea of how the garments must look on the runway.

You also have such refined and surprising productions . . . Do you use a runway show designer to help you develop your ideas?

I wish! But I have very clear ideas and work side by side with my assistant in the projects.

Could you give us a rough estimate of the budget for one of your runway shows?

You should never talk about money!

Who is your audience?
We simply prepare it and hope that people come. We try to make it simple. We prefer events open to the public. Since there are so many people involved, it's good that they can invite their friends and contacts. At times, it's not possible to invite everyone, although I would like to. It depends on the size of the place where we hold the show. For the last runway show, the audience could buy tickets to sit in the front row.

Which runway show has been the most difficult to carry out?
They are never easy and we are always so busy creating the installations that we need for the show. Especially, because the installations are so big and play a major role in the show. The Solar Donkey Experiment was particularly difficult as it did not only involve people. Haha.

Is the runway way show a key element for a designer?
I think it is extremely important so that people can understand you as you can fit the collection into the surroundings where you can imagine it and if you wish, tell a story along with it.

How do you see runway shows in the near future?
I hope they become more and more open and they do not only involve a select group of people. More music, more people, more animals and more inspiration.

LEFT The Human Laundry Service runway show produced for the fall-winter 2009 collection. **TOP** Presentation of the Fantabulous Bicycle Music Factory collection for spring-summer 2008. **BOTTOM** Presentation of The Big Wet Shiny Bobbies Collection for the spring-summer 2007 collection © Photographs by Alastair Wiper, courtesy of Henrik Vibskov.

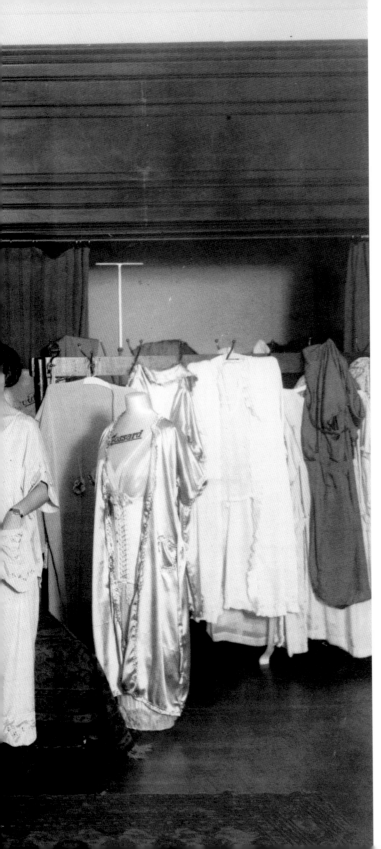

Background

Let's take a short break and go back in time to see how things used to be done and discover the origin of the runway show. Everything has a beginning, even runway shows. It occurred at a specific time for a specific purpose. It wasn't down to chance. In the beginning, the models were not especially beautiful, tall or worshipped. They were the girls who ran around the shops holding up the heavy mirrors in which the elite of society tried to find their best profile. Naturally, these girls began to model the outfits that the designer wanted to propose to the clients, who seated in a comfortable parlor, projected their images onto those walking heads imagining the dresses that they would wear to their next charity ball.

Runway show in the twenties in Wells Shop, a store in Washington specializing in corsets and hats. Image from the National Photo Company Collection. Original negative LC-F8-6877 from the USA Library of Congress.

It all started here

In the dances held in the sophisticated ball rooms, ladies and gentlemen fought to sit in the front row to view the attire of the guests. Watching, observing and judging were the pastimes of high society. In this voyeur game lies the reminiscence of the runway shows. This was also the case in the beauty contests organized to decide who was the prettiest among all the candidates. According to historian Valerie Steel,[1] the beginning of runway shows is uncertain. Most agree that the first hints of a runway show as we know it today were made by Charles Frederick Worth, considered as the first couturier at the end of the 19th century.[2]

Until then, tailors and seamstresses worked to the demands of their clients, who gave them the ideas, the fabrics and the details. Charles Worth revolutionized the creative process by fabricating an unprecedented production system: he devised the creations in advance with fabric and details of his choice, and his clients were limited to choose from the models, which would be then tailor-made.

This new understanding of fashion involved a new way to display it, hence the birth of the runway show. It seems as though Worth was the first to demonstrate the movement of the fabric on the body using models. By invitation only, he showed his collection to his clients in luxuriously-decorated parlors where young models would show off his creations.[3]

At the start, the clientele, who were used to him coming to their homes and reluctant to lose the exclusivity in an event that gathered together several clients, were unenthusiastic about the new format. But the insistence and resilience of Worth made them change their mind, and soon his shows became an exclu-

LEFT Lady Duff Gordon fitting a model with an evening gown in her studio in New York in 1916. Photography courtesy of Randy Bryan Bigham. TOP Engraving published in 1777 by Darly that belongs to the British Cartoon Prints Collection of the USA Library of Congress. Entitled *The Back-Side of a Front Row*, we can guess that the runway shows connected a long tradition of court events in which everyone aspired to sit in the privileged front row.

sive date in the busy schedule of high society.

The models in these days were not especially tall or beautiful. They had to simply model the garments and walk in a straight line.[4] The girls, also known as so-sies, were chosen by the buyers or the assistants who held the heavy mirrors. Marie Vernet stood out among them. Vernet was considered as the first model in the history of fashion, and years after her debut she married Worth, which contributed to his success.

The presentation of the garments in succession one after the other and collections regarded as an ensemble of unified guidelines also have their origins in the illustrated pages of the fashion magazines that showed the proposals for that season of the different dressmaking shops. This iconography was transferred to the parlors, where the figurines were transformed in real models who showed the latest fashion trends.

The first runway shows

The first runway shows are related to the theatre and they were developed at the same time as the movie house. The parallelism that historian Caroline Evans[5] made between the runway shows and the value of movement during this period is interesting: "There are visual similarities between the effects of the 'still image' of a row of models in a show and the human silhouette in the movies. Movement in relation to time and speed seemed to capture the same essence of modern life in both art and business. The same imperative stimulated the runway show: a desire to materialize modern living rather than merely represent it."

The Parisian designer Paul Poiret was the first to design a presentation exclusively conceived for the press in the summer of 1910. The models organized by the couturier modeled two in two and the event was specifically designed for a reporter and a photographer that a few days later was echoed in an article titled "Une leçon d'élégance dans un parc" (a lesson in elegance in a park) published in the newspaper *L'Illustration*.[6] Lady Duff Gordon, the English aristocrat behind the label Lucile, actively participated in this founding stage with sophisticated events that she organized in her stores. In a space conceived as a show room with expressive lighting, live music and not-to-be missed programmes, the models, baptized with exotic names, modeled under the instruction of Lucile with proud and theatrical poses before a select public.

Lucile self-proclaimed she was the originator of the runway show, and although not all historic fashion books agree, they do recognize her contribution.

Lucile used the knowledge she acquired designing the wardrobe for musicals and West End shows to transform her showroom on Hanover Street into a mini theatre. "It had a soft, luxurious carpet that covered the large showroom and beautiful matching, grey brocade curtains hung on the windows," she explains in her notes. "At the far end of the room there was a miniature stage, with olive-colored gauze curtains in the background, which created the desired effect." To reinforce this production, Lucile contracted six models, six "glorious, goddesses [...] who were capable of doing her work justice."

After a hard training regimen that included trips to the hairdressers and long hours walking with books on their heads, these girls became the "incarnation of femininity."[7]

To complete the total metamorphosis of the models, Lucile rebaptized each one of the girls replacing "their incongruent names (working class) such as Susie and Kathleen Rose for more exotic names such as Gamela, Dolores and Have, in keeping with the individual personalities of each of the models." Although Lucile was not the first to contract models to show clothes, she was definitely one of the pioneers in exploiting their potential as actresses and their sex appeal. Lucile's theatrical runway shows soon became the talk of London's high society, and the business of the de-

signer took off. "When the lights changed and the music played and the models walked down the runway, there was no woman in the room, whether she was fat or old, who did not think about modeling those clothes that the beautiful, thin girls were wearing. And this was the prelude of the purchase".[8]

The indisputable star of the runway shows was Lucile herself: when she came out onto the stage to sell her garments, her authority status in fashion shows was confirmed.

The twenties

During the twenties, runway shows were a major social event, and they were celebrated in the designer's parlors, in sporting arenas or large warehouses. The models walk slowly, without saying a word and never looking anyone in the eye with the clients seated in the audience listening to the designer's explanations of the collection.[9]

A second generation of seamstresses such as Paquin, Doucet, The Callot Sisters, followed by Chanel and Poiret, established their labels in the first few decades of the 20th century converting Paris into the fashion center of the world. Jeanne Paquin, who can be considered as one of the pioneers in fashion communication, converted her runway shows into flamboyant events, holding them in theatres. She also sent her models to the most popular fashion events, such as the Longchamp horse races, so that they could flaunt her creations.

Coco Chanel encouraged her models to adopt a unique and individual posture that is now a cliché: hips forwards, shoulders back, one foot in front of the other, hand in pocket and the other one making gestures. According to Chanel, gestures and attitude were what brought life to her garments and years later defined her own individual and unmistakable style.

Jean Patou conducted one of the first castings when he exclusively selected white, American females to model his creations. This selective use enabled his clients to identify more easily with his garments and helped the modeling profession become more socially accepted.

In the USA

While in Paris the runway shows spread around showrooms and were carried out behind closed doors exclusively for the social

PARIS FASHIONS 1912.

elite, in the USA large department stores had their eye on the French capital and it was these stores that organized the presentations of the collections imported from France before large crowds. Sellers from all over the country put on runway shows, including restaurants at lunchtime. These runway shows became very theatrical and it was normal for the pieces to be modeled along to the voice of a narrator. Edna Woodman Chase, who organized in 1914 one of the first runway shows in the USA (Fashion Fête), said in 1954 that runway shows had become a way of life.[10]

The new look of Dior

The presentation of The New Look collection by Christian Dior in 1947 was a turning point

LEFT Two girls who attended the Longchamp horse races in 1912. George Grantham Bain Collection. USA Library of Congress. **RIGHT** Coco Chanel with her studied pose at home. 1929, Faubourg, Saint Honoré, Paris. Photography by Sasha/Getty Images.

in the history of fashion and a change in the format of runway shows. "Unknown the day before," writes Françoise Giroud, "Christian Dior becomes an instant celebrity."[11] Marie France Pochna immediately places us in the designer's presentation when she transcribes the testimony of the Vogue editor Bettina Ballard:[12] "The first model appears, and the whirlwind of her skirt sends the ashtrays flying. One, two, three models follow with immense energy to offer an inedited and careful theatrical representation that manages to surprise all present."[13]

Until then, the major dressmakers presented their clothing in a peaceful and tranquil manner, in silence, and only with the voice of the house's representative in-

dicating the corresponding number.[14] Dior made his models act and give life to his garments with a rhythm of dizzying movements while he presented the models with imaginative names.

The fifties and sixties

In 1949, the expression prêt-à-porter is born, adapting American fashion based on large-scale production. The new culture of mass production and a better standard of living means that after the Second World War the desire for fashion expands through all social classes, converting it into a universal phenomenon. At this time, fashion designers specialized in prêt-à-porter who worked for the label as a creator, designer, stylist, coordinator, controller of the gar-

ments in the production process and even a salesperson for their own products.[15]

In this context, the British designer Mary Quant made her models dance and run to the rhythm of jazz during a tour in a hotel in Switzerland. It was a surprise for all those who attended the gala dinner.

In France in 1966, Paco Rabanne with a runway show entitled "12 Experimental and Unwearable Dresses in Contemporary Materials", Pierre Cardin with a runway show called "Happening" that took place in the street, and Christiane Bailly with a crazy presentation in which the models drag a line of vegetables to match the color of their miniskirts, all bring a breath of fresh air in comparison to the classicism that prevailed in the traditional prêt-á-porter presentations.[16]

Media runway shows

In 1970, the Japanese designer Kenzo inaugurated the era of the media runway shows with a presentation in which the runway extended to the stage, the audience was four times the normal size and the models had a carte blanche to improvise.[17] During this decade, the prêt-à-porter shows grew in size and two models—Jerry Hall and Pat Cleveland—emerged as the goddesses of the runway and introduced their profession to the star system. The top model was born.

The production of the show took on a major importance and the figure of the runway set designer emerged.

Norbert Schmitt and Bernard Trux "conceive the runway as a show based on the strongest themes of the collection, in which the prologue and the end play an important role, and they choose the music and the models."[18] They were the first in the profession to achieve recognition in the press.

In the eighties everything was done in style. The runway shows were televised on cable or satellite, the press filled the presentation, and champagne flowed backstage. In 1984, Thierry Mugler celebrated his tenth anniversary; he presented his fall-winter 1984-1985 collection organizing the first public and payable runway show in France, which 6,000 people attended in Zenith in Paris.

In the eighties, Versace was invited to join the haute couture calendar to bring a bit of oxygen to a fading sector. Until then, the norm was to hold the shows in show-rooms, in front of a select guest list of no more than two hundred guests. However, Versace opted to do things differently. Instead of holding the runway show in his showrooms, the Italian designer used the pool of the Ritz Hotel, he covered it with a monumental runway and crammed the front row with VIPs.[19] He converted his presentation into the most talked about date in fashion. Gina Bella-fonte explained in the magazine *Time*: "Gianni Versace hastened the transformation of fashion from a rarefied interest of the elite into an object of bottomless mass cultural fascination."[20] Houses such as Chanel, Valentino, Alaïa and Armani competed to seduce the media and fans competed to seduce the media and fans, cast-ing the best models, who became authentic celebrities and making major investments so that the show could go on.

The other side

Far from the shining lights, from European aristocracy and from the large budgets, a few miles from Paris, fashion was stirring up a revolution. Punk defined London as a new fashion capital and an-archy and individuality were the maxims. Caryn Franklin from *i-D* magazine said in the book *Cat-walking* by Harriet Quick: "It was all about individuality. Design-ers were really reflecting club and street culture and they found their models on the street, clubs or among friends. I remember going to the Paris collections and think-ing: is this all the models are going to do? Just walk up and down? Of course, that was the norm."[21]

Vivienne Westwood merged the rebellious style from the street with tribal funk and Victorian couture attracting a legion of fans and receiving rave reviews from day one. A new way to understand a collection, a new way to pose, a new way to model. This breath of fresh air from London inspired newcomer Jean Paul Gaultier, who with his designs mocked contemporary culture and he mixed several atypical characters from the world of fashion along with the models such as transves-tites and tattooed people.

Ode to the concept

The first Comme des Garçons runway show in Paris represent-ed one of the last suggestions to dress the current panorama of typologies and formats of run-way shows that coexist. In 1982, a runway show where bare-faced

LEFT Martin Margiela surprised everyone with his first Japanese-themed runway show. For the presentation of his first spring-summer collection in 1989, the models shoes were dyed red leaving a trail on the large white sheet spread over the floor. With this fabric, a jacket was made for the next season. © Photography by Raf Coolen.
RIGHT Hussein Chalayan has created, show after show, an appropriate and individual manner to exhibit his collections. Three to six models usually wear his most conceptual outfits, defining the concept around which the collection is based. In the image, the Afterwords spring-summer 2000 collection presentation © Photography by Chris Moore, courtesy of Hussein Chalayan.

models walked down the runway to cacophonous music managed to break the conventionalities and infuriated the press, who compared Rai Kawakubo runway show with the Hiroshima tragedy. The Japanese designer, who has even been accused of degrading the image of females, wanted to reject this bourgeois notion of clothing as an element to seduce, and used fashion as a way to provoke ideas, integrating the model as part of the message.[22]

Six years later Margin Margiela presented her first runway show, in which the models had their heads covered and their shoes dyed with red paint, walking on a white sheet that was then used to make a piece for her second collection.

In 1999, Hussein Chalayan presented Echoform, a runway show with high political and conceptual content during London Fashion Week. The burka as a piece of clothing was fragmented to show the models completely naked and wearing only a mask.

The runway as a show

In the nineties, haute couture fell into the hands of British designers such as John Galliano, who first of all designed for Givenchy and later for Christian Dior, and Alexander McQueen, who took charge of Givenchy. Until then, journalists had not spoken much of haute couture as there were few readers who could access this select fashion division. Six months later, the haute couture runway shows reached a high level, and they managed to attract more publicity than the prêt-à-porter runway shows. Taking one step further than Versace, Galliano and McQueen embarked upon large scale productions where their work was showed to a large audience and in which the productions and the art management were as important, if not more, than the actual beauty of the garments.[23] The extreme theatricality of these shows is interpreted by Caroline Evans as "a pretext to disguise its commercial origins and goals".[24]

New technologies

In 1995, Walter Van Beirendonck

transformed the runway into a virtual experience when the models interacted with computer-generated images. A little more than ten years later, Kate Moss, the model of the moment, opened an Alexander McQueen show in the form of a hologram. In 2009, Viktor & Rolf presented their first runway show broadcast online with only one model, and Stefano Pilati presented his menswear line in an audiovisual format with a short movie simultaneously projected on three large screens. The designers became familiar with the broadcasting of their presentations using streaming. Burberry, Michael Kors and Isaac Mizrahi took the first steps. Alexander McQueen offered in fall 2009, after much anticipation, the first live broadcast of one of his runway shows. He promised then to bring his followers on journeys you've never dreamed were possible.[25] Even though on this occasion the experiment was not a total success because the server overloaded, meaning that a large part of the audience could not access the event, it was clear that fashion had reached a point of no return.

A future in the fourth dimension

The current economic climax has forced many of the big labels to control their investments, and, as a consequence, presentations have gone back to their origins, leaving the theatricality for big occasions and producing more effective and austere runway shows. Christian Lacroix, one of the few survivors of haute couture, abandoned the calendar and is placing importance on more economic presentations. The future is uncertain but, without a doubt, the Internet takes the shape of a large window where anything is possible, and it is likely that many will decide to exhibit their detailed and luxurious collections with its help.

Thierry Dreyfus

Art director
www.thierry-dreyfus.com

Thierry Dreyfus has many years experience working with runway shows, first of all as lighting designer and a few years later as an art director with the company Eyesight. He worked along side Hedi Slimane in his years as an art director for Dior Homme and together they devised impressive and refined presentations in which the light plays an important role. Passionate, perfectionist and blunt, he creates an emotional and authentic show blatantly rejecting fashion that is based on marketing and numbers.

What role does light play in runway shows?
Light is a powerful tool that transforms reality. If you are out and about, everything is lit up; light determines the ambience of a space. Light helps to highlight certain elements of a collection and creates a precise atmosphere. For example, if your collection is predominantly black and you want the models to appear ethereal, light can achieve this. Helmut Lang has always worked with a certain type of light, daylight, convert-

can work up to twenty hours per day. I believe it is important to work with designers that offer a personal touch. I have no time for those who are only interested in marketing. Names such as Hedi Slimane, Helmut Lang or Consuelo Castiglioni have their own personality. Helmut Lang, for example, has a very personal focus, the same identical and personal concept that identifies the label. In 1993, there was not as much emphasis on marketing, but now everyone is too worried about putting on big

Runway show celebrating the 40th anniversary of Yves Saint Laurent in the Pompidou Center in Paris 2002.

"Now younger generations seem to be obsessed with fame, but what is important is that they do something: express themselves not just to be in the front row. They need to forget about fame"

ing it into the trademark of the house. It is important to take into account how the photographs will turn out, what angle they will be taken from, etc.

What is your favorite part of producing runway shows?
I consider myself as a craftsman. My passion consumes me and I

shows, this does not interest me in the slightest.

What is your working method with designers?
I like to talk directly to the designer. Without any middlemen. A lot of the time we exchange images. Architecture, painting, photos, etc. to be able to pre-

cisely define the lighting and aesthetics of the show.

What is your main goal as art director?

My work consists of achieving a scrupulous, in-tune and coherent result in line with the philosophy of the label. If someone comments on how incredible the music or the light is, we have done something wrong. It is important to explain the theme in a clear and reliable manner. I still remember when Jean Paul Gaultier told me in his tattoo runway

show: "Imagine the light in Morocco in the sixties. You know what I mean?" It was difficult to achieve but we got there.

Where do you get your inspiration from?

There is not one source of inspiration. I love to visit museums with paintings from the 18th century. I am a big fan of Goya and I love the Greek silhouettes.

Is there any particular runway show that stands out for you?

I remember a Martine Sitbon

Helmut Lang 2004. ©-Thierry Dreyfus

Fashion weeks

And you, where do you hold runway shows? New York, London, Milan and Paris are the big names in fashion weeks; they are the only locations that can aspire to hold the most flamboyant, expensive and exclusive runway shows as well as the most alternative, fresh and ground-breaking. Each of these cities, with their own personality and moments of either more or less glory, attract journalists and specialized magazines that help to feed and build this cosmopolitan image. The reasons behind this privilege are not down to chance, and many designers with an airfare, dream and suitcase know that they must catch a plane to take off.

The calendar

Designers begin to create their collections six months before a public runway show and a year before they reach the shops. Paris, New York, London and Milan coordinate their calendars so that the buyers can supply their stores with products for the next season and the press can cover the consecutive events.[1] Planning and distribution are very important for a line to be successful. If you can show a collection first, a better level of distribution can be achieved. For this reason, putting together a fashion calendar responds to a complicated commercial operation and forces the designer to meet delivery times, working under pressure and quickly.

During February and March, the fall-winter collections are shown, and the spring-summer collections are shown in September and October. The menswear fashion calendar is held one month before and the haute couture runway shows have their own position in the calendar. The capitals readjust their calendars season after season without an exact date to be able to offer a competitive agenda to buyers and reporters who have to cover all the shows.

Until recently, the market had traditionally defined two seasons per year (spring-summer and fall-winter) with the objective to supply new products when there was demand and to achieve return on stock control.[2] In recent years, the rigid division between the two seasons has become diffused with the introduction of new dates on the traditional calendar to allow for the presentation of pre-collections and capsule collections. Capsule collections work independently from the calendar. They respond to a specific marketing need and consist of six to ten pieces designed around a very specific

LEFT Illustrator Gi Myao draws sketches during Paris Fashion Week. Here, the spring-summer 2008 collection by John Galliano for Christian Dior. TOP The line-up of girls before the spring-summer 2008 runway show by Josh Goot in New York. © Photography by Sonny Vandevelde.

Presentation of fall-winter collections[3]

....

January
Prêt-à-porter men's runway shows, haute couture runway shows, pre-collections

Hong-Kong Fashion Week, Milano Moda Uomo, Paris Men's Fashion Week, Paris Fashion Week (haute couture), Mercedes-Benz Fashion Week Berlin

February
Prêt-à-porter female fashion weeks (New York, London, Milan, Paris)

Photo session for the fall-winter campaign, photo session for the fall-winter lookbook

Oscars, BAFTAs, Golden Globe Awards

Copenhagen Fashion Week, Mercedes-Benz Fashion Week New York, London Fashion Week, Cibeles Madrid Fashion Week, Buenos Aires Fashion Week, Milano Moda Donna

March
Prêt-à-porter female fashion weeks (New York, London, Milan, Paris)

Photo session for the fall-winter campaign, photo session for fall-winter lookbook, press conferences to show the fall-winter collection, lookbook distribution

Paris Fashion Week (prêt-à-porter female)

April
Presentations of the fall-winter collection for the press

May
Cruise collections, Cannes Film Festival

....

June
Pre-collections, Milano Moda
Uomo, Paris Men's Fashion
Week

July
Preparation of the Christmas
press releases, preparation of the
St. Valentine press releases

Prêt-à-porter men's runway
shows

Haute couture runway shows

Mercedes-Benz Fashion Week
Berlin, Hong-Kong Fashion
Week

August
Copenhagen Fashion Week

September
Prêt-à-porter female fashion
weeks (New York, London,
Milan, Paris)

Photo session for the spring-
summer campaign, spring-
summer lookbook distribution

Mercedes-Benz Fashion
Week New York, London
Fashion Week, Cibeles
Madrid Fashion Week, Buenos
Aires Fashion Week, Milano
Moda Donna

October
Prêt-à-porter female fashion
weeks (New York, London,
Milan, Paris)

Press conferences to show the
spring-summer collection

November
Press conferences to show the
spring-summer collection,
Easter press releases

Paris Fashion Week (prêt-à-
porter)

concept and that, when combined, can create about twenty different outfits. On the other hand, pre-collections, in pure effervescence, work as an advance of the main spring-summer and fall-winter collections. Their origin can be associated with cruise collections, spring-summer pre-collections that were traditionally designed to satisfy the demands of high society, who in the height of winter traveled to exotic holiday locations. Currently there are designers who also present fall-winter pre-collections.

Previously, it was during the fashion weeks when buyers made their orders; however, now it is in the pre-collection meetings when designers manage to sell 70% of the collection. The pre-collection is normally made up of a few simpler and more commercial versions of the garments that a few weeks later will be shown on the runway. The presentation of this collection is held in the showroom and it is aimed exclusively at buyers and a very small segment of the press.[4] This type of presentation responds to the need to facilitate the task of buyers and to increase the production rotation in stores.

The consumer, who is more and more informed and demanding thanks to new technologies, continuously demands new products throughout the year, in addition to the normal rhythm of the runway shows around the world. A six month wait seems eternal, and for this reason the possibility of buying some garments that will be modeled on the runway a few weeks later is extremely attractive. Also, the seasons are diffused, and it is not odd to see girls wearing a light summer dress over some thick tights in the middle of winter, and consumer uses have been globalized. All these factors contribute to the flexibility and continual updating of the fashion calendar.

From the traditional two seasons, the market now demands at least four seasons. For this reason, many companies regularly produce six collections. Companies such as Zara and H&M that have a different production system, supply their stores every two weeks with new products.

It is normal that magazines publish their pre-collections and begin to dedicate space to them. Designer Peter Jensen presented in June 2009 his first cruise collection and so thoroughly enjoyed the experience ("I had so much fun, sharing a cup of tea with my guests and giving everyone a chance to understand

my brand and the clothes close up"[5]). that he decided to use a more simple runway show format for his new spring-summer collection 2010.

Faced with this frenetic rhythm of demands, some small designers have said enough is enough and they have decided to produce as they like regardless of the demanding and unreachable system with short production periods, which can only be achieved by large companies with a strong logistics system.

The Big Four

Four capitals have become geographical centers with their designers and presentations that fill magazines and shop windows around the world. New York, London, Paris and Milan, each one with their own role are known as the Big Four. The press is partly responsible for these four capitals holding the exclusivity and leading role in fashion production. *Vogue* magazine has had a specific role in this matter. The American edition of *Vogue* was founded in 1892 but it focused solely on fashion from 1909. The London and Paris editions followed in 1916 and 1920, respectively, and it was not until after the Second World War that the other international editions such as the Italian and Australian editions appeared.

The magazine became an object of desire that gave advice on what was in vogue way beyond Paris, London, New York and Milan. However, the world represented in *Vogue* was practically limited to these capitals until recently, when they began to feature events that

TOP AND RIGHT The end of the runway show by Riccardo Tisci for the fall-winter 2009 runway show by Givenchy in Paris. © Photography by Gerard Estadella.

ran parallel to the major cities. Naturally, designers choose the city where they are based, but many, for strategic reasons and in search of a market that accepts their pieces, aspire to hold shows in one of these four cities.[6]

Paris, the capital

"You may be considered a genius in London, but if you want to acquire a truly international status, you should hold a show in Paris. It has been like this from Worth to McQueen."[7] This is the president of the Fédération Française de la Couture Didier Grumbach's opinion on the relevance of Paris as a fashion capital.

The fact that Paris holds this position is not down to chance. The city offers tradition, protection and the infrastructure so that a designer can comfortably develop

and support their career. For this reason, many designers choose the capital to set up their headquarters and showrooms.

Paris runway shows are organized by the Fédération Française de la Couture, which was established in 1973 and it is currently headed by Didier Grumbach. This Federation offers apprenticeship plans for young designers, the representation of French fashion abroad, the creation of synergies among members of the industry, and protection against intellectual property rights. Divided into three labor union associations (haute couture, female prêt-à-porter and male prêt-à-porter), it is the Fédération Française de la Couture that creates the runway show calendar, allocates locations and decides which reporters will cover the event.

In the seventies, the Fédération Française de la Couture decided which designers should hold shows in nearby locations in order to give the public a general perspective of the designers' creations and make the reporter's work easier.

In order to be able to hold a runway show in Paris it is necessary to be a member of the association, and admission is decided in terms of the company's business results: volumes of sale, actual potential and international projection. Candidates should send a letter to the labor union association, which will then send them an application form that should be filled in and completed with a press album.

The support of a sponsor or patron can be decisive for the admission into the elite of design-

ers and so that the candidature is brought before the selection committee.[8] The supremacy of Paris in the calendar is indisputable, on the whole because it is the only city capable of holding the most traditional and refined designs as well as the most alternative and avant-garde proposals, paying special attention to the value of fashion as a creative and expressive resource.

The inaccessible exclusive runway shows, their dazzling lists of guests and the extreme professionalism in everything presented are features that augment this legend.

London-born designers such as Vivienne Westwood, Alexander McQueen, John Galliano and Hussein Chalayan never hesitated to present their collections in Paris, which gave them a carte blanche in their creativity and a solid business structure.

Milan, the tradition

The Italian style was conceived, in the opinion of Pamela Church Gibson, under the mythology created by the press and Hollywood itself, and Rome, being the capital, played an important role in this promotion.

The structure of Italian industry is a far cry from the Paris or London industry. Its strong point does not lie in haute couture, but in top-quality prêt-à-porter collections. Between 1971 and 1978, the most established Italian designers abandoned Flor-ence for Milan. At the same time, a new generation of enterprising designers who had started out their commercial and industrial adventures in the North of Italy chose the same city to become established.[9]

Organized by the National Chamber of Italian Fashion, founded in 1958 with the objective to assess and defend the interests of its members, Milan Moda Uomo and Milan Moda Donna have held throughout their history some of the most spectacular and lavish runways shows in the history of fashion. The Made in Italy campaign continues to be a guaranteed success for labels such as Armani, Prada, Marni, Versace, Gucci, Etro and Moschino, and tradition, luxury and quality are the trademarks of one of the runway shows most frequented by buyers. Far from competing with the creations in Paris, in 2000 an agreement was signed along with the Fédération Française de la Couture to establish a shared exportation policy in countries that are not part of the European Union. With over 230 runway shows in each of its editions, 2,500 accredited journalists and 15,000 buyers, it continues to be a benchmark, in particular in the menswear sector.

London, a breath of fresh air

Organized by the British Fashion Council, London Fashion Week has become a reference point for the youngest, most confident and irreverent proposals. The designer Mary Quant showed that the latest trends in London could be very different to those in Paris. Faced with the soundness of the French model, Quant filled magazines with her

Chelsea girl, a model of a woman who was defined by her youth, her slender body, her confidence in the city and her confidence to experiment with a variety of looks.[10] Vivienne Westwood took the baton with her risky presentations far from the trite paths. Twenty-five years later, the British capital continues to offer a breath of fresh air year after year and strengthens its position in the powerful Big Four circuit.

The creativity in the London Fashion Week is not down to chance but the result of strong support, from the outset, of the youngest designers and the creation of solid bridges with fashion schools across the country. NewGen is a sponsorship programme created in 1993 from which designers such as Alexander McQueen, Boudicca and Matthew Williamson have benefited, and Fashion Forward is a competition for enterprising designers that has a substantial cash prize.

The only "but" that many specialists put forward about the potential of the British capital as a capital that generates fashion and new talents is its incapability to offer British designers a solid industrial structure with which they can build a label and survive the hardship of the economy. It is for this reason that many of the most loved designers have moved to Paris.

New York, a style of its own

In New York, the runway is sponsored by a maker of cars and it is entirely organized by an individual company, IMG, specialized in high caliber media events. Previously known as Press Week, it was the first fashion week in history. Founded in 1943, the event was designed to move the attention away from French fashion during the Second World War at a time when it was impossible for journalists, buyers and experts to travel to Paris, and it familiarized editors of magazines such as

Vogue and *Harper's Bazaar* with native designers.[11] Later, London and Milan adopted this same formula and offered their designers an overall framework where they could show their collection. Exclusively aimed at prêt-à-porter collections, the New York Fashion Week, on account of the importance of the American version of *Vogue* along with its media director Anna Wintour, has gained ground in the last few years and has managed to cross the Atlantic and awaken interest in the European market, which traditionally has focused on its own runways.

The institution that is home to and supports the designers is the Council of Fashion Designers of America (CFDA), a non-profit organization that has about 250 members. Founded in 1962 by the designers themselves, new members can join by invitation only and they must have at least three years experience. Their sponsorship and awards pro-

The Daily is a publication created specifically for the London Fashion Week where you can get behind-the-scene information. Design created by Jenny and the Cat Ltd and published by the British Fashion Council by RUBBISH Ink Ltd.

gramme CFDA/VOGUE offers opportunities to the youngest companies and those with most future potential.

Beyond the Big Four

In recent years, and on account of new technologies and the coverage in alternative forms of media, the four large fashion capitals have seen how cities such as Berlin, Copenhagen, Vienna, Rio, Antwerp and Sydney have managed to position themselves in a notable second place, showing that there are other interesting proposals outside the circuit and traditional formats.

LEFT Anna Jagodzinska opened the presentation of the fall-winter collection 2009 of American designer Zac Posen. Here she poses in her second outfit of the night for the backstage photographer © Sonny Vandevelde. **RIGHT** American model Coco Rocha (Elite NY, www.coco-rocha.com) poses with a copy of the paper *Daily Front Row*, published during New York Fashion Week and edited by the online publication team *Fashion Week Daily*. Photography courtesy of Mercedes-Benz. Michael Buckner/Getty Images.

The reasons are varied, but many buyers seek alternatives to diversify their offer with more economic proposals to complete their most exclusive orders. The press, in particular due to the Internet boom, has detected certain demands from its readers to learn more about what is happening beyond the traditional circuit.

The small city of Antwerp is a curious case and worthy of being studied. Its streets have seen the birth of designers such as Ann Demeulemeester, Martin Margiela, Dries van Noten, Walter Van Beirendonck and Dirk Bikkembergs, who with their innovative designs are known as the Antwerp Six and have managed to put their city on the fashion map. They have inspired a new generation of interesting and promising designers such as Bruno Pieters, Bernhard Willhelm, Olivier Theyskens and Véronique Branquinho, who currently design between both Antwerp and Paris. The school of visual arts La Cambre in Brussels and the Antwerp Royal Academy of Fine Arts are also jointly responsible.

The recently created Berlin Fashion Week managed to attract the attention of the reporter Suzy Menkes, who dedicated an enthusiastic title to it: "Berlin Fashion Week Shows a Raw Energy." The fact that this runway along with Copenhagen shares sponsors and management with New York has contributed to the media interest of these emerging events.

Outside the calendar

Newcomers and promising designers normally present their collections outside the official calendar, which is called "off schedule," in alternative presentations that often are not as costly. Some acclaimed designers also feel comfortable in a more independent and individual context.

An off-schedule presentation offers the advantage of total liberty in choosing location, date and time. In contrast, attracting the attention of the media and buyers is more complicated. Therefore, it is important to size up and study the date so that it does not overlap with other important events.

Runway shows in schools

Some schools believe that, from an educational point of view, holding a runway show is for graduating students the culmination of their studies. In recent years, the British Saint Martins College or the Fashion Department of the Antwerp Royal Academy of Fine Arts runway shows have managed to achieve good press coverage, eager for new talents, and even for some designers this runway has resulted in the start of a career. For four years the webpage *Style. com* has been describing on the same level as with other shows the graduation runway show of the Saint Martins College to offer the scoop about first steps of future fashion talents.

In 1984, John Galliano made his debut on the graduation runway of this school with a collection entitled Les Incroyables that received rave reviews in the press. Joan Burstein, owner of the London-based fashion stores Browns, remembers: "It was a moment I will never forget. He was Saint Martin's best-kept secret."[12] Blown away by this first collection, Burstein bought the entire collection and dressed her windows with it immediately.

Graduate Fashion Week has been held in London since 1991. It shows the best work by graduates from schools all over the country, without a doubt a good opportunity for those who studied outside London.

Although runway shows and similar initiatives were organized in many cities, London is the connection between schools, press and professionals.

The reporter and lecturer Sue Jenkyn Jones offered in her book *Fashion Design*[13] some useful advice for students who were preparing their graduation runway show: try to choose a simple concept. It is also important to visualize the desired effect: will the models appear one after the other, two in two, or in a group? Will they walk fast or slow? Will they remove any clothing or will they pose at the end of the runway? Also, the introduction of curious features works well, as long as they have been organized in advance and planned with due order to achieve the maximum effect.

Michael Brow

Set designer
www.lot71.com

Michael Brown is a run
signer. He is in charge
a magical and surprising
the runways so that the
etched in the minds of
After graduating in His
and Architecture in the
versity of Providence, it v
until he realized that his
in scenography with the
creating visual stories.
ing in more than two h
ater, opera and runway p
in 2004 he founded Lot
in charge of designing ar
form the brand identity
spatial experiences. His
include Chanel, Gucci, (
gari, Loewe, Yohji Yamar
my Hilfiger and Hugo B

What is a runway show for you?

A runway show is like watching a private showing of a musical videoclip, it is an ephemeral moment: for 10 to 15 minutes, the collection of the season shows unperturbed elegance, glamour, beauty and charm accompanied by images, vibrant music and lighting fitting of a rock concert. Organized for the photographers' snapshots and lookbooks, a runway show also should transmit the identity of the label and the spirit of the designer and his/her collection.

In your opinion, what does a runway show require to be remembered?

I strongly believe that the chosen space has an exceptional power when creating an experience. Recently, we have worked to create experiences for the spectator; we have built

a visual and auditory story that will amplify the collection in a short and intense lapse of time. The presence of design in the assembly, decoration, lighting, music, the images and the choreography all define a place that serves as a visual context of the collection.

What are the five key elements for a runway show to be a success?

One of the first elements to take into account is the location. How the models enter and the backwall are equally important. The set design must act as a support and enhance a collec-

tion, improving and enlarging its spirit and identity.

What does your job as a set designer entail?

Working as a set designer for the fashion industry is rather creative. Normally, a fashion label or a production agency

"The set design must act as a support and enhance a collection, improving and enlarging its spirit and identity"

hires me. My main function is to create the atmosphere and the set for the productions. At first, I meet with the client to gather information on the collection and to carry out the creative management lines. Then, I elaborate visual documents in order to discover the set design language that best suits the project. After reaching an agreement with the client on the visual language, style and tone of the runway show, I develop the storyboards. From these initial drawings and along with the client, the production agency and other designers we create the definite drawings. The next step is to prepare a report specifying the entire construction process, and the materials and finishes of each element. When the moment arrives to turn the sketches into a reality, I am present throughout the entire construction and installation process, supervising that all the decor is built and designed as it should be.

What is your creative process?
My inspiration varies depending on the label and the collection. For research, I observe and analyze: photographs, sculptures, buildings. Some of my clients are very clear when expressing the creative vision of their collection. Others only give me sketches and samples of the collection. I understand the design process that I carry out along with the client as a partnership: we work in a team to create a visual story, an experience designed around clothes. I also draw inspiration from the collection, the designer and the location where the runway show will be held.

What are the most important features when designing a set?
The photographers must take good snapshots of the collection. This, along with the fact that the set design must evoke the spirit and the identity of the collection to suitably transmit it to the guests, are the two most important aspects when designing a set. The third key aspect is to convey good energy and an unexpected surprise, both when the model walks out onto the runway and at the end of the show, I always seek to design a

deceitfully intelligent set, a landscape that tells a story about the collection and communicate it subliminally to the guests.

Approximately, how much does a set for a runway show cost?
If we are talking large scale, the budget would be between 100,000 and 300,000 dollars. Currently, due to the economic crisis, there are not as many magnificent runways shows being produced, currently I work with budgets varying between 25,000 and 100,000 dollars.

Are there any designers that you haven't worked with that you would like to collaborate with?

I would love to design the set for a Marc Jacobs runway show. His are large-scale, evocative, theatrical and provocative presentations and of course I like his style. In the future I would like to work on more projects outside the USA, especially in Paris and Milan as they require more creative and theatrical set designs.

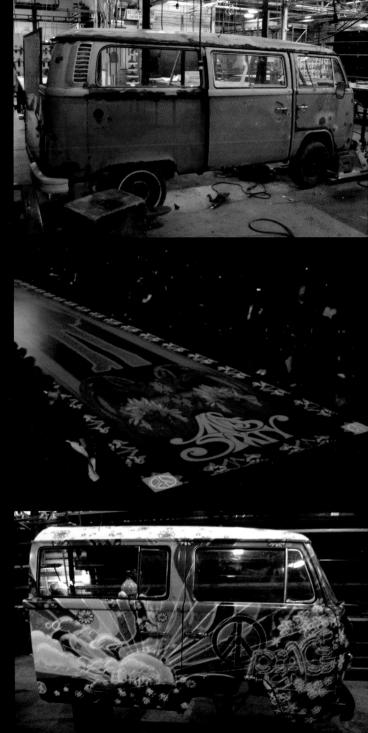

Details of the Michael Brown creative process for the production of the fall-winter 2008 Miss Sixty show. © Photography by Michael Brown.

The formats

A case for an outfit. From the most exaggerated Baroque style to pure minimalism, the diversity of ways to design a production and create a sense of movement within is wide-ranging. Who are we, what do we want to tell, and who do we want to aim it at: these are questions that we must ask ourselves to determine the language to communicate with future clients. The attention is focused on random locations, and discovering the best way to attract attention with regards to our idea is fundamental to begin to imagine and create in our minds these ephemeral spaces that enshroud the outfits for barely fifteen minutes.

The OMA architects studio presented an avantgarde innovative choice of location for the presentation of the menswear spring-summer 2010 Prada collection. A select and reduced public could view the runway show live, the other spectators watched it through small windows designed for them. On the wall, dialogues of male cinema characters. © Photography by Marco Beck Peccoz, courtesy of OMA.

Types of runways shows

Marta Camps established a typology of runway shows in her piece of work "The elements of a runway show".[1] Taking into account her testimony and that currently formats are being redefined, we are daring to offer more updated, modern versions.

Press runway shows

Press runway shows are held within the context of fashion weeks or off-schedule to exclusively show the collection to the press. These runway shows are designed especially for press editors who sit in the front rows and photographers who are located in an area normally reserved exclusively for them at the end of the runway, as it is very important that they study the area and take the best image that will later be featured in the press. On many occasions, these images will be used for communicative purposes, such as on the website or the lookbook, a graphic element aimed at buyers and press with photographs of the entire collection. These runway shows create great expectation: Will they use supermodels? Who will sit in the front row? What music will they choose? These are the questions many fashion editors ask themselves as soon as they open the invitation.

Within this type of runway shows, we can distinguish between haute couture and prêt-à-porter runways shows.

Haute couture runway shows

Haute couture runways shows aimed at the press are exclusively held in Paris. They were traditionally held behind closed doors. However, the arrival of Versace to the haute couture sector, instigated by the Federation itself in order to give a breath of fresh air to a static sector, opened the curtains and took the collections out of the showrooms to show them

LEFT The production company Villa Eugénie managed to recreate a street scene with great fluency for the fall-winter 2009 collection by the Belgian designer Dries van Noten. The pallet of colors used by the designer perfectly matched the grey and urban setting of the space. © Photography by Patrice Stable, courtesy of Dries van Noten **TOP** The Grand Palais de Paris holds one of the most awaited runway shows of each season, the Chanel show. © Photography by Sonny Vandevelde.

in luxurious locations with a production concept similar to that of a concert, theatre or the opera. The most important feature of this type of runway show is its elevated budget that can cost up to one million euros.[2] The investment normally is recouped owing to the media coverage that these types of presentations generate. The promotion achieved as a result of the runway show is not directly recovered from the sale of the collection but indirectly in the sale of its perfumes, sunglasses or bags, which are more accessible for the public as a whole.[3] Bernard Arnault, director of the LVMH group has publicly recognized haute couture as a key factor in the success of the Christian Dior label. Its designer John Galliano has a carte blanche in his runway shows, which function as a means of communication which, more than simply showing the product, generates a stimulating dialogue between the press and Dior.[4]

Prêt-à-porter runway shows

The prêt-à-porter runway shows are different from haute couture for the type of collections that are shown. They are made up of garments that are mass produced in standard workshops and that six months later can be found in high street stores. The prêt-à-porter collections are more affordable than haute couture collections but the costs generated by the runway show, the advertising and the use of high-quality raw materials and series, not mass, production make their garments expensive objects that often belong to the luxury sector. The majority of buyers cannot access runway shows, and to get information on the collections there is nothing better than checking it out online or flicking through the fashion magazines.[5]

Showroom runway shows

Showroom runways shows have a more austere production and are aimed at a smaller public, in particular the buyers, who can appreciate the creations of the designers and decide what items of the collection they will purchase for the following season. These shows can also be directed at a select group of press. Media runway shows have been the choice of the majority of designers in recent years. However, with the growth in popularity of pre-collections, recently some labels have begun to organize smaller runway shows and presentations in the showroom. These types of shows are similar to those that were held years ago in private showrooms for the most elite designers. Currently, for the larger labels, there are more exclusive clients and special buyers who deserve a private pass. Hedi Slimane, who boosted the status of menswear fashion from his time at Dior Homme, tells in an interview for *Hintmag.com* that when he first landed a job in YSL, he pro-

LEFT In the Sonia Rykiel runway shows, the models forget about the forced poses and model smiling freely. In the image, the runway show for the fortieth anniversary of the label, which was held after a lively gala dinner with a guest list crammed with known faces. © Photography by By2photographers, courtesy of Villa Eugénie. **RIGHT** For the debut show by the designer Kris van Assche in Dior Homme, he decided to forget about the runway and opt for a more intimate presentation. In order to do so, Thierry Dreyfus and the Eyesight production agency created a luxurious Parisian setting with crystal chandeliers, mirrors and careful lighting. © Photography by Marie Drouin, courtesy of Eyesight.

posed a small presentation of this type: "It was only two models in twenty looks set in an 18th century French salon. It was shown to only about five people, including Suzy Menkes, Carine Roitfeld, Hamish Bowles, Jim Moore from *GQ*, and editors from *Le Figaro*. It was really nice, really haute couture style. It was very prudent that I didn't start right away with a big show. I needed time to develop it. I had to first make it known where I was going."[6]

Celebrity runway shows

Celebrity runway shows are directed at the end client, who by flicking through magazines or channel-surfing hears or reads about Dior, Balmain, Lanvin, Hussein Chalayan and even Martin Margiela. Actresses, singers, aristocrats and politicians become special models however they are showing off their outfits with every public appearance. With studied and stylish poses they model, whether it is on the red carpet or drinking a tea on Sunset Boulevard, the designer's latest creations. Images are, then, spread like wildfire, and within a few hours an unknown designer is the talk of the town.

Audiovisual runway shows

In recent years, the runway has opened a window to the fourth dimension and audiovisual supports have been chosen by many designers to complement or improve the presentation of a collection. If a while ago this choice was risky, currently it is an economical, efficient and accepted alternative by the press. But the first few attempts are always complicated. Bradley Quinn explains in his book *Techno Fashion* [7] that the designer Julian Roberts found all types of inconveniences when he decided that he only wanted to show his collection in an audiovisual format at the start of 2002. Roberts, familiar with audiovisual language and who often puts on shows during London Fashion Week decided that he wanted to do things differently: "London has the reputation of being an innovative place with a wide array of interesting fashion. However, designers continue to show their collections in the same way as they do in Paris, New York and Milan. We need more." So he made a film about his new collection and decided to show it during Fashion Week instead of producing a runway show. As the British Fashion Council did not recognize the audiovisual presentations as a legitimate form of a show, it was difficult for him to finally present the collection

as he wanted to. Roberts pointed out that the lower cost of this format as well as the flexibility in its broadcast would popularize its use. And he was not mistaken.

A few years later, an unprecedented decision was taken in a renowned house; Stefano Pilati decided to substitute his YSL menswear runway show for an audiovisual format produced by Colonel Blimp. The video, a format associated with the most alternative designers and one that created reluctance among the more conventional press has become institutionalized as a valid format and today it is a normal format that companies use to present their collections.

Virtual runway shows
Virtual runway shows are aimed at the end consumer, the press and buyers, all of whom are sat in the front row at home. In 1996, the designer Walter Van Beirendonck imagined a futuristic alternative to traditional runway shows and launched his collection on an interactive CD, converting the runway into a virtual experience in which the models with their futuristic looks modeled in a virtual world of computer generated images.[8] On this occasion, the CD became a common way to present collections. A decade later, in February 2008, the designers Viktor & Rolf go one step further and present the first ever online runway show. The runway show was considered as "a take on what a fashion show might be in the future"[9] and the instigators prayed that democracy had finally arrived. For more than fourteen hours, the model Shalom Harlow modeled twenty outfits on a long

TOP Audiovisual features have accompanied presentations in recent years. In the image, the presentation of the spring-summer 1998 collection that Martin Margiela produced in collaboration with Comme des Garçons in which a collection of short one-minute movies with live explanations of each of the ten pieces in the collection. © Photography by Marina Faust, courtesy of Maison Martin Margiela. RIGHT The producer Colonel Blimp was in charge of producing the audiovisual presentation of the menswear fall-winter 2008 collection by Stefano Pilati for YSL starring the actor Simon Woods. The audiovisual format became a regular in the most established labels. Photography courtesy of Colonel Blimp.

runway located in the showroom of the designer's virtual house. Several cameras and showings showed the garments in detail from all angles. The result was condensed into a seven-minute video that could be viewed on the designer's website in a worldwide presentation that anyone with Internet access could view. On 6 October 2009, Alexander McQueen along with the online magazine *Showstudio*, offered the live broadcast of his Paris runway show on a webpage created exclusively for the occasion, permitting all fans to participate in this special event. Days before, all the fans arranged a meeting on Twitter. Expectations were high and it was so successful that owing to a server overload, only a few could enjoy the show.

The genres

Within the world of runway shows, regardless of who they are aimed at, several genres have been shaped out over the years through which the designer builds up his/her identity and communicates a certain style at the same time. The media impact of some has converted them into platforms through which some designers, in addition to exhibiting their collection, also disseminate ideological and personal character messages. Choosing one type or the other will largely depend on the type of collection, the runway selected to hold it, the budget as well as the type of public who will attend. On some occasions, the types juxtapose and the varieties mute and diffuse with regards to the specific needs.

The classic runway show

On a simple runway, the models clearly show the designer's garments, which are lit up specifically and are subject to the rhythm of the music for fifteen or twenty minutes. The designer's sole objective is to present the collection in a clear manner without any additional messages that distract the buyer's attention.

Within this genre, the novelty comes from elements such as position and location of the runway, the format of the runway (which can be square, circular or double-row), the choice of specific lighting and the use of a certain type of accompanying music that conveys a certain type of emotion that matches the collection. The presentation is developed within the classic canons: the lights are turned on, the music begins to

play and the models begin to walk one after the other down the runway, stopping at the end, they pose while the photographers capture the precision of the outfits, turn around and then disappear behind the curtain.

When all the outfits have been shown, the music stops and the spotlights are turned off. The lights are turned on again and all the models appear in a line behind the designer, who comes onto the stage to greet and thank the public. The outfits shown on the runway are practically the same as those that the buyers can find in the showroom. Calvin Klein, Donna Karan and Lacoste are labels that opt for this type of classic presentation.

The theatrical runway show

Halfway through the nineties flamboyant runway shows came back en vogue, both in Paris and London, which some are known as "the new performance."[10] The designers realized the commercial value that the show created to attract both the press and the buyers.[11] The production was dramatized with decor appropriate to an opera show and is accompanied by narration. The main objective is to impress and seduce.

The runway shows by the British designer John Galliano are utterly theatrical. The seduction conveyed through the shows since his first performances allowed him to increase his resources and establish a certain style, using more and more theatrical techniques, such as replacing classic lighting on the runway for more theatrical lighting or choreographing minute by minute each model who walks down the runway three days before the presentation also giving clear guidelines to models who, only wearing one outfit and not changing the design throughout the night, not only model but

act. The existence of a narrative with a common theme allows the designer to articulate and give the runway show a sense of meaning, which is developed from the moment the first model steps out onto the stage until a finale loaded with emotion. The beginning, middle and end of each fictional production are reproduced on a small scale for a mere twenty minutes that a runway show may last. In the Suzy Sphinx runway show, Galliano showed a punk dream-like schoolchild, a lover of the movies and ancient Egypt who from her native England was transported from Egypt to Hollywood, where she interpreted Cleopatra in a movie. Accompanying this fantasist digression, the runway becomes a stage and is home to spectacular productions that give meaning and credibility to the stories that are told on it.[12]

In this type of runway show, many of the pieces that are used in the presentation are only produced for the show and the collection in the showrooms and stores is much less flamboyant and more wearable. For example, one of the most stunning gowns by Alexander McQueen, made from over two thousand small rectangles of glass, which took over six weeks to make, featured for a mere two minutes on the runway and after the show, only one version was ever worn in public by Bjork in concert.[13] In this case, the dress more than accomplished its function: to be photographed on the runway and in sophisticated fashion productions, to become a trademark for the designer that will remain in the retina of those who will later enter a store and recognize it on the label of one of his garments.

The conceptual runway show

Conceptual fashion and its production, just as conceptual art, is not held back by shapes or materials but by ideas and concepts.[14] Through this type of runway show the designer presents, communicates and questions, inviting those present to reflect on certain aspects or themes. Hussein Chalayan is a designer who bases his runway shows on the basics of conceptual art; Claire Wilcox defined his runway shows as "art installations."[15] According to Chalayan, the concept is as important as the outfits, and their presentations are close to a performance if they are not already a performance. The runway shows are a way to invite the public to think about religion, the body or the woman's position in society and these types of reflections are essential for the creative process.[16] The case of Hussein

Chalayan is also interesting to see that although the designer constructs his pieces and runway shows with artistic language, this does not mean it is art or that it enjoys the liberty that art does. One of his first presentations, in which guests were invited to reflect on the meaning and sense of the burka, caused major controversy. The designer had to mold and moderate his discussion in order to not hurt people's feelings. Far from ideological debates, Chalayan continues to reflect on universal themes.

Martin Margiela is another designer who likes to break preconceived ideas and who uses clothes and his presentation as a vehicle to express himself. His first runway shows were different from conventional presentations in four basic points: his collections were not new each season, but often redefined old pieces, as well as using recycled garments; many of his models were not professional, he selected unusual locations and rejected any notion of one person taking over the show, referring to himself as part of a team. Regarding his presentations, the expectations of the audience were systematically broken, like when he showed the collection in total darkness, which was only broken by illuminated umbrellas that his assistants, dressed in white coats, carried. It is interesting to observe that from the outset his radical and groundbreaking ideas have been adopted by other designers and they have now become more normal than innovative.

Designers like the German Bless, the trio Three as Four from the USA or the Belgian Bernhard Willhelm are other names that stand out for their conceptual approach to both collections and presentations. Even designers such as Marc Jacobs, who is accustomed to more conventional runway shows and a more referential working method, surprised everyone with a fun conceptual runway show to present his spring-summer 2008 collection. Here, Jacobs reflected on the pass of time and the order of the things with a runway show in reverse order: he was the first to appear and then the models. The order of appearance of the outfits was also altered and the outfits shown on the runway also played with this idea.

Juxtaposition of genres and types
Though very different types of runway shows have been presented,

LEFT AND RIGHT The space used where the models show off the collections can come in many shapes and sizes. In the image, the OMA proposal for the spring-summer 2009 Prada collection. Photography courtesy of OMA.

the combination of these genres is not uncommon. In a classic runway show, a small audiovisual piece can be projected or a spectacular set can be built. Likewise, concept and dramatic quality can coexist in one presentation.

Collaborations and synergies

It is not uncommon in runway shows for the designer to collaborate with artists who give a certain added value to the presentation to up the interest of the press, surprise the audience and strengthen their positioning on the market. Whether it is using a famous face in the casting, using a current group to play the accompanying music live or selecting a renowned producer to direct the production, in runway shows collaborations and synergies are very popular. In the eighties, Trussardi contracted the horror movie director Dario Argento to produce a show in which the models where apparently assassinated with a knife and thrown off the runway. Lily Allen sung live at the Chanel haute couture runway show and the architect Rem Koolhaas, from the OMA studio has been collaborating for years with Prada creating interesting productions for their runway shows.

Frédéric Sanci

Sound illustrator
www.fredericsanchez.com

Music is one of the essen
ents in a runway show, a
Sanchez has a special se
providing music that pe
picts the designer's out
did not exist that exactly
work, so he made one up
lustrator. He compiles n
of a collage of music that
cally creates for each ru
Frédéric draws imaginary
the Marc Jacobs, Calvin
and Rue du Mail presen
erything began with the
Margiela runway show in
a new way to conceive
shows and their music.

You define your profession in the runway shows as a "sound illustrator". Could you go into a bit of detail about this concept?

When I started in 1998 there was no title that defined what I did. I am not a musician but I'm not a DJ either. Music can tell you a story and that is what I do: I tell stories using music. For this reason I chose this name, it's a bit more poetic and the term musician seemed a bit limited to me. And in a way, I have paved the way for others to use this expression.

How do you work with the designer to develop the music for the runway?

I often work with people such as

tions of the collection. They give me a lot of leads. Normally, I start to work two weeks prior to the runway show; I have many clients that I have worked with for many years and have forged a good relationship with them and this speeds the process up. First of all, we have a conversation in which we try to create images that then need to be transformed into music. I try to make the music translate these images and I try to recreate them while the models are on the runway.

Give us a practical example.

A year ago, for the spring-summer 2009 collection by Marc

Frédéric Sanchez provided the accompanying music for the first Maison Martin Margiela runway show, a moment to remember. Photography courtesy of Maison Martin Margiela.

"In a minimalist production, music becomes a virtual element, evoking images and transporting them to certain moments and spaces"

Marc Jacobs or Miuccia Prada. I like to talk directly to the person; it's the method that works best for me when I have to create music. I like to see the outfits, but at times it is better to look at the moodboards, they help me absorb all the inspira-

Jacobs we were trying to hit upon the sound track for the runway show. His collection oozed styles from the thirties and forties as well as the first designs by Yves Saint Laurent. We had to find something that connected these two concepts and

...hat would work. So we came up with jazz. However, it had to be a type of music that suggested something cliché from New York that was popular and sophisticated. So we finally chose *Rhapsody in Blue* by George Gershwin, which is a perfect mixture of jazz and classicism. So we went down this line and we used this one type of music.

Does it take you long?

Usually one week is enough to create the accompanying music for a runway show.

Suzy Menkes said that music feeds fashion. How important is music in a runway show?

In a runway show, music has a very different role to what it has in a theatre or in the cinema. In a minimalist production, music becomes a virtual element, evoking images and transporting them to certain moments and spaces. There are no physical images but music is there to be able to create them mentally.

Have you worked with many dif- *ferent types of designers? I imagine that there are many different ways to work…*

Each label is different and each one has its own way of working. With some I can experiment more than others. Prada, Marc Jacobs and Martine Sitbon are very creative people with many concerns. I don't work with people who are obsessed with the commercialism; I like people who create things.

What was your first runway show?

The Martin Margiela runway show. Then, I was not especially interested in fashion. I was young and was looking for work in the media but that involved different disciplines. And fashion has a transversal character, bringing together elements such as theatre, dance and cinema etc. In the eighties, there were figures such as Peter Saville who designed record sleeves and who began to work with Marc Ascoli and Yohji Yamamoto: this type of mix was what interested me. At this time, apart from

the Japanese, there was something retro about fashion. The runway shows were a replica of what was occurring in haute couture houses. When I met with Martin Margiela we wanted to do something really contemporary and we chose music that had never been previously used in fashion.

A much more aggressive style of music and from the start to finish it was the same thing. The nineties were much more creative.

And what now?

Well, now it's a bit like the eighties … If you watch recent runway shows, they have the same format as the one I created along with Martin.

On many occasions it is difficult to recognize the music used in a runway show…

This does not worry me, for me the most important thing is that the message is understood and what least worries me is that the spectators know what the music is. I love when I am flicking through magazines and find, along with the collections of the designers with who I have worked, some of the images that we have used to create the music. This means that the message has been understood.

Do you think it is important to have a good economic means of support to produce a first runway show?

You can do many interesting things in a studio. We have done it. You must be creative and imaginative. Marc Jacobs began making T-shirts, so . . . why could you not be the next big name? Another question is that your objective is to become the creative director of a big label. In this sense, my opinion is that the goal must be something big and different, and you must find new ways and paths. In short, it is important to be creative in your own way.

Marc Jacobs runway show. © Photography by Mark Reay.

From the idea to the budget

For all tastes, colors etc. The production, models, combination of items, accessories, music, lighting, makeup, invites, etc, everything involved in the preparation of a runway show involves taking speedy decision on many different matters. Each small choice is a new input of information that is added to the overall meaning of the general line. The inputs, which are legible and easy to identify, will make sense when, juxtaposed, they are part of a coherent and compact line where it will not be necessary to decipher or explain anything. With a mere glance, those seated in the front row will understand what we want to say.

A model poses for the spring-summer 2007 Vivienne Westwood Gold Label in Paris. © Photography by Daniel Mayer.

The briefing

On many occasions, the seed of what the runway show will turn into is established even before the collection's items. Designers, along with their producers, begin to create runway concepts three to six months in advance, the general guidelines that the label wants to follow in the following season are drawn up in this phase. During the development of the collection, new inspirations emerge that can come from many different areas and that will gradually frame the final concept of the presentation. Visual and audiovisual references from movies, television, music and art are often the most used sources of inspiration for designers and the art directors who help to produce a simpler visual format to understand better what the designers want to say. In short, they must have their eyes wide open at all time, know how to observe and digest the referents intelligently. In the spring-summer 2009 runway collection, Hussein Chalayan wanted to convey the speed with which our lives move and along with this idea the hair stylist Eugene Souleiman created some spectacular hair styles based on images in the sporting press that freeze during a moment of high speed. US designers Rodarte used far-reaching inspiration for the leitmotiv of the collection as the starting point to visualize the space where the fall-winter 2009 collection would be presented: the land art of the seventies, the installations with Robert Smithson mirrors in the seventies, the Sun Tunnels by Nancy Holt and the cult movie *Donnie Darko*[1] were the references that art director Alexandre de Betak

LEFT The designer Bruno Pieters adds the finishing touches to the first outfit of the fall-winter 2008 collection that the model Iekeliene Stange will wear on the runway. © Photography by Sonny Vandevelde. TOP Backstage at the Vivienne Westwood runway show, the photographer Daniel Mayer creates an improvised moodboard with Polaroid shots of Pamela Anderson, the face of the label for the fall-winter 2009 season. © Photography by Daniel Mayer.

brought together in a mysterious and conceptual installation. For others, ideas come to them when working on the actual collection and creating the pieces and many agree that the majority of ideas come from the most daily activities. Starting points can be very random, depending on the designer. Some creators provide specific and precise ideas in each of the runway production studios, while others only offer general guidelines. Alexandre de Betak has been producing John Galliano runway shows for the last ten years and when he is asked about the work process with the Dior designer, he explains it all starts off with few words. Galliano declares sex and danger or perhaps he prefers danger and romance and then the ball starts rolling.

The document explaining the designer's guidelines and, in short, the working tool for the producer or the art director, is the briefing. It is vital that this document can be easily read because if something is misunderstood, it can have a negative effect on how the collection is viewed by the press. The collection itself communicates one message however when external elements are introduced, it alters the meaning and is interpreted differently. For this reason, it is important to consult and exchange ideas with the team without taking things for granted. What do we want to convey? Will it be understood? Is the collection coherent? Does it complement or neutralize the outfits? These are some of the questions we must ask ourselves when drawing up the document.

Art director Thierry Dreyfus explains that the concept to be developed for the spring-summer menswear Dior Homme runway show was very specific: Kris van Assche represented a breath of fresh air in the house and for this

reason he turned the runway into a magnificent stand covered with dark canvas that, when the music started, the canvases fell one after the other until it was filled with natural light. In this way, the show went from the darkness of Hedi Slimane to the luminosity of Kris van Assche, in a production filled with symbolism. Designers compile and express their inspirations using moodboards, a collage of illustrations and ideas on a piece of card that brings together different sources of inspiration: the attitudes, the colors and the type of lighting are jumbled and used as a reference to start to work on

and communicate the idea. The art director, lighting designer, makeup artists and the team involved normally exchange ideas to make the concept more tangible and this builds up a dialogue between all parties. According to Thierry Dreyfus, it is necessary to see the collection before deciding on the lighting requirements: what colors predominate the collection, if the material is transparent and how the models move are all aspects to take into account.

Drawing up the budget

First of all, designers must figure out their budget and how it

is going to be distributed. This will largely determine the scale of the presentation. The cost of a runway show can vary from the 10 million dollars that a media-obsessed flamboyant Victoria's Secret lingerie runway show can cost to 30,000 euros for an independent designer. The average stands at 150,000 euros, a figure that for many is unattainable and for this reason there are sponsorships that offer the possibility of producing meticulous but much more austere presentations. The Rodarte designers have managed in a short period of time to awe the press and place themselves up there with the best US designers.

LEFT Backstage in the spring 2009 haute couture runway show by Christian Dior, the model Natasha Poly getting her hair styled. © Photography by David Ramos. RIGHT The casting director for the Rue du Mail runway show, the label Martine Sitbon label takes some Polaroid shots of the model lekeliene Stange. © Photography by Sonny Vandevelde.

Their runway shows are professional and of a high-quality but they have a large number of sponsors from Lexus Hybrid Living to Mac, who provides equipment and material and Aveda, who provides the hair stylists. Winning the award from The Council of Fashion Designers of America in 2006 valued at 50,000 dollars also gave the label a boost. For other designers, forming part of the international circuit, which means appearances in influential magazines, is a major economic effort.

To draw up a budget, several items must be taken into account:[2]

EVENT EQUIPMENT. This item should include the fees and expenses of the art director, who is the person who actually designs and makes the set design, the stylists, who will combine the different outfits lending them coherency and personality, the casting directors, who will choose the models, the models themselves and the dressers who will help them to dress backstage (often they are students who volunteer to work for free). On some occasions, due to a lack of budget (the production of a Parisian runway show alone can cost between 28,000 and 139,000 euros) an art

director and stylist are not used, however this should not affect the quality of the runway show.

Depending on the amount of outfits in the show, a certain number of models must be contracted and this will determine the number of changes that each one of them has to make throughout the show. Choosing the right models is not an easy task, and for this reason many designers contract a casting director that will carry out this job. Here, there is no room for error so that the runway show can proceed calmly and with no major mishaps: a miscalculation could cause an imbalance of the

models on the runway, and there is nothing worse than an empty runway. Not all models know how to walk on the runway, therefore it is necessary to select models with experience and also not all of them have the same fee: their fee will depend on their popularity in the world of fashion and their availability. A well-known model may be a major lure but this can really bump up the budget. In the nineties, Versace paid 50,000 dollars for the then top-model Christy Turlington to exclusively model for their runway show. Fortunately for designers, the top-model era is over and currently a model with a high fee can charge 15,000 euros per runway show, of which the agency keeps 20% commission. Minimum fees stipulate 500 dollars, but models who are just starting out charge a minimum as the runway show in

question can be a launch pad for their career.

TECHNICAL EQUIPMENT. This should include the cost of music, which may vary significantly depending on whether a professional musician composed a piece of music especially for the occasion, or if a DJ plays a short set during the show or if a choir provides the accompanying music. The lighting designer and equipment will create the desired atmosphere and will decide what quantity of light and the material to be rented for the event. Although the press will immortalize the event, it is important to contract an in-house photographer and a video team that captures the most interesting aspects so that this material can later be used in the catalogue, in the lookbook and on the website. Rodarte designers hired the

TOP Final touches to the models minutes before the fall-winter 2009 runway show of the French label Léonard. © Photography by Eric Oliveira. **RIGHT** Two dressers help a model in the Antonio Marras runway show. © Photography by Eric Oliveira.

photographer Autumn de Wilde, specialized in indie music portraits, to photograph the backstage and line-up in an individual and more personal way. These images can now be seen on the website. Choosing a good make-up artist and hair stylist, who are used to managing a team and working with tight deadlines, is also essential. The technicians who will work with the music, lighting and art team, the safety and transport are other expenses included in this expense item.

MATERIAL. Each of the members of the art and technician team will need material to carry out their work: hiring out the location, the material for the set, atrezzo, hiring out the required lighting, accessories etc. It is also necessary to think about the catering, the construction and execution of a backstage area with tables, mirrors, lighting so that hair stylists, make-up artists and models can work as comfortably as possible. Also insurance must be taken out that covers certain losses or damages.

COMMUNICATION. Part of the budget must be reserved for all the necessary communication material for a runway show: on the one hand there are the invitations, apart from the actual production costs, the graphic designer's fees who designs the piece and the cost of sending them to the mailing list must be considered. Also the photographs for the press dossier are another cost included in the creativity and production costs. Many designers, apart from the press dossier, give out a small gift, as a way of showing their appreciation to those present; it may be a scarf, perfume, bag, etc.

If the designer opts to give out a gift, this should also be accounted for in the budget. On some occasions, the designer must cover travel costs and allowances for some of the press members and celebrities. There are so many elements that must be considered for this short production and for this reason alone many designers outsource part of the work to a production agency who will take charge of coordinating the different teams and will give the designer an overall estimate covering all items. All costs must be assessed to get an exact figure of the cost of a runway show.

Choosing a suitable format

Choosing a suitable format is essential to honestly communicate the collection while at the same time being loyal to the label's philosophy. John Galliano with his spectacular and voluminous historic-style garments chooses a theatrical, sumptuous and vintage format to show his collections. Hussein Chalayan, with his conceptual, architecturally-constructed pieces stages them in minimalist spaces with atypical presentations. Julian Roberts, with a small budget but many ideas, opts for an audiovisual presentation. All of them have polished and perfected their presentations and modified their choice in line with their reality, their clients and always being conscious of their resources. It is important to be clear on who we are, to convey it with clarity, precision, in the most appropriate and suitable way. An event that best fits your requirements will be designed by taking into account the available budget and the parts of the show that need to be highlighted according to the philosophy and identity of the label. On many occasions, the lack of budget forces designers to use their inventiveness and think about alternative proposals to both reduce costs and achieve certain notoriety.

Chris Kelly and Sara Flamm made their debut in 2007 at London Fashion Week with the name Théâtre de la Mode, they attracted attention with an unusual presentation of miniature mannequins, a more modern version than those used by 19th century tailors, dressed in their outfits to present the collection. The accessory designer Devi Kroell presented her first prêt-à-porter collection in an austere and delicate way in the renowned Milk Studios in New York with a group of models who were placed in an installation built for the occasion placing the focus on the garments. The Barcelona-based designer Cecilia Sörensen took advantage of the virtual Future Tense platform, a window created by Showstudio through which upcoming designers could express their creativity through a moving image. A short movie entitled *Inside Out* was produced to present her spring-summer 2009 collection. Instead of trying to fit in many different economical elements which will detract from the quality of the show, it is better to simplify and invest the budget wisely with the idea of complementing the collection. The lighting director Thierry Dreyfus is unequivocal in this sense: "If you are a young designer, my advice is not to produce a runway show. Hire out a showroom, ask a few friends to model for you and try to strike up a relationship with the press."[3] In this case, the bud-

get would go towards hiring out the showroom, hair stylists and make-up artists, designing, producing and sending out the invitations as well as monitoring the press and guests. If the designer did not live in Paris and they wanted to get to know the city of fashion, traveling expenses and allowances for the team for the couple of days in the city should be taken into account.

Contrary to this, designer Hamish Morrow made a commercial decision to do runway shows for a few seasons, however he would not produce the collection until he had built a reputation for himself.[4]

Meanwhile, Erin Fetherston, in her first collection did not put on a runway show, but instructed the photographer Ellen von Unwerth to produce a short movie starring her friend Kirsten Dunst who showed the collection and which succeeded in drawing media attention. Chris Kelly and Sara Flamm from Théâtre de la Mode do not doubt for a second that the budget plays a major role when selecting the format: "Understanding the financial implications of presenting a catwalk show, we wanted to take a new stance on contemporary fashion. One that allowed us to enter the fashion world without compromise and in turn reach a broader audience of fashion and art connoisseurs alike."[5]

Timing

It is also important to establish an activity schedule so that all team members can work with a certain deadline, suited to their activity. Many designers begin to think about a new runway show as soon as the last one finishes. Meetings with the production team start three to six months before the event. After the first brain-storming meeting, it is likely that they exchange ideas by phone or by email (taking into account that many of them travel and have very tight deadlines). In this initial phase, it is essential to convey in detail the ideas that they have in mind so that the art director, the stylist and the casting director can translate them. It is about being specific so that professionals can get the right idea. Next, the sketches with the ideas will arrive, the 3-D models, opinions will be exchanged and

the ball will start rolling. If the designer agrees, the art director will begin to order the material that very day, which he/she needs to construct the runway where the girls will model. A month or two weeks in advance the casting director will hold a one or two day conference with the models, either in the designer's offices or in the showroom. Their measurements will be taken, they will be asked to do a trial run, the director will have a look at their book and they might even have to try on some of the designer's garments. All the material will be sent to the designer, who will assess which models best fit into his/her style and will decide, along with the team and the stylist, which outfits best suit which models.

One week before, once they have decided on what outfits will be presented, fittings will be held where the models will be assigned and then try on the outfits in order to see how the outfits flow when moving to try to adjust the clothing best to each model. The accessories will also be decided and hair trials will be carried out. A few photos of each style will be taken. One of the face and another full body shot. The full body shots will be hung on the cards where each model has a changing area and which contain the instructions for the models outfits and dress changes. The other photo will be used to create another card showing the order that each model must go out onto the runway.

A few days before, the workers begin to construct the stage. Many pieces will have been prepared weeks before in the production workshops. There is a lot of equipment and hiring out space is expensive so more often than not the set is built on that very day. Fitting the lighting, covering the floor, ordering and arranging the seating requires a large, coordinated team. The day of the runway show, a tight schedule forces all members to work against the clock. Hair stylists and make up artists begin to work four hours before the runway show. It is normal that some models, the most sought after, arrive at the last minute and need to get ready quickly. Halfway through make up and hair styling, music, lighting and

LEFT Kim Noorda backstage in the Marc Jacobs runway show. © Photography by Sonny Vandevelde. **RIGHT** Tanya Dziahileva enters the backstage in a rush in the Giambattista Valli runway show. © Photography by Sonny Vandevelde.

choreography of the models are tested. The trial run is crucial to check if there is anything missing. After the make up and hair is done, the dressers begin to dress the models in order of who goes out onto the runway first. In some cases this order is indicated on the floor. The stage manager and production team will bring order to the backstage area controlling that each of the processes is completed in the correct time frame.

Jean-Luc
Dupe

Press officer
www.systeme-d.net

He is the middleman b
designers and the specia
trying to convert that un
able name into a univer
the fashion industry. Spe
modern menswear fashic
made his debut workin
Xavier Delcour, Sébasti
and Romain Kremer.
to-date and on top of a
trends, Jean-Luc tells us
Twitter the demands of t

is there are other ways to present a collection to buyers and to the press. However, a runway show is probably the most impressive way to do it, although this also involves styling the outfits, something that not all designers are good at.

How much can a runway show cost?
From zero to a thousand billion euros. Of course, there is a minimum cost for the space, production, lighting, sound, video, equipment, models, hairdressers and makeup, printing and sending out the invitations, etc. In addition, the budget can vary considerably depending

remember that a bad production can give a bad impression. So I would say the minimum cost of a runway show would be roughly 10,000 euros.

In your opinion, what format is most suitable for a runway show?
Mainly, a format that works best for you and reflects the personality of the designer or the label. In my opinion, the more synthetic the better. Professionals see a large quantity of runway shows every day and I think that a runway show has a lot more impact when it is concise and has one direction, demonstrating powerful individual ideas

"*Someone who feels that they are not seated in the correct position will probably not assess the*

the selection is made also in terms of the target, the communication strategy, the image of the label, the marketing or the development plans. For example, there is no need to invite the most fashionable magazines to attend a commercial runway show, unless the label is an advertiser in this publication. Next is the delicate theme of seating, that is, how to position the most important people and those who most support the label in the best seats.

Is the front row so important?
With regards to celebrities, most

rio, they may leave before the show even starts.

What advice would you give to a designer preparing their first runway show?
Make it simple, brief and not repetitive, and always be honest with yourself. If you are going to show your collection in a fashion week, remember that your audience will probably attend more than twelve runway shows per day. If you want them to remember you, don't bore them. They are professionals who know what to look out for and how to dissect the runway show.

Russia and Portugal. I particularly remember a summer runway show in the mid-eighties by Claude Montana in the Cour Carrée du Louvre, first of all because it was the first show that I attended, and also because the marquee was enormous, it was crammed with people, a sea of photographers fighting for the best photos, poised feature models of the eighties and masses of shoulder pads and Montana leather. The second that stands out was a runway show by Alexander McQueen in 1996 and his magical universe. The art direction and the set design by Simon

Images taken by Jean-Luc Dupont during the preparation process of the spring-summer 2010 Masatomo runway show. Some of the images were uploaded to Twitter to share them live with followers of the label.

How do you see the future of runway shows in times of the Internet?
Currently more and more people prefer to view runway shows on Internet, quietly in their house and with a glass of wine instead of queuing for half an hour, squabbling for a seat and waiting quite a while for the show to begin. Runway shows still make sense and are necessary but I also think that we need the help of the Internet, and perhaps the designer should think of other ways to show their collection apart from the conventional runway shows.

Teamwork

An experienced, informed and coordinated team can be the secret to success. Far from the tranquility of the workshop, a fashion show is an event that, despite its short duration and its ephemeral nature, involves a great deal of professional and logistical and economic resources. A group effort of producers, makeup artists, hairdressers, stylists and lighting designers who are all passionate about their profession and work side-by-side. Careful planning will help them to realize its full potential. Together they will build this little unique mirage that truly reflects the soul of the collection, the designer's philosophy and spirit of the moment.

Minutes before the spring-summer 2009 haute couture runway show by Elie Saab there is still a lot to do. © Photography by David Ramos.

Giving life to ideas: art production
As previously mentioned, many designers opt to hire a production company to be responsible, after organizing a briefing, for art direction, managing all the logistics, coordinating the team and suggesting the professionals that will be needed to produce the runway show. These agencies offer a range of services including finding the location, the planning and construction of the production and technical teams and managing the safety equipment, backstage, and the general production of the event.

Normally, behind a big runway show is a big production company with whom the designer works regularly and is able to understand, process and recreate their needs, adding in the personality, tastes and expectations of the creator.[1]

Behind the stunning Alexander McQueen runway shows is the production agency Gainsbury and Whiting, led by the efficient Sam Gainsbury and Anna Whiting. Their clients include Stella McCartney and Christopher Kane, and they are now one of the most successful production agencies in the UK. In Paris the production of runway shows is distributed between four companies. Behind La Mode en Images is the oldest producer of all, Olivier Massart, with twenty-five years of experience and who organizes Balenciaga, Louis Vuitton, Kenzo and Valentino runway shows. The lighting and artistic director Thierry Dreyfus, meanwhile, regularly works with the production company Eyesight to create runway shows for Dior Homme, Jil Sander and Sophia Kokosalaki. Based in Brussels,

LEFT Image from the Dries van Noten spring-summer 2009 show. © Photography by Patrice Stable, courtesy of Dries van Noten. TOP A steward beside the paper creations made by Stéphane Lubrina for the spring 2009 haute couture collection by Chanel. © Photography by David Ramos.

Étienne Russo, the alma mater of Villa Eugénie, designs Parisian runway shows for Chanel, Dries van Noten, Lanvin and Hermès. And Alexandre de Betak, who the press quickly associates with Cecil B. DeMille or Federico Fellini for the magnificence of their presentations, organizes runway shows for Christian Dior, Viktor & Rolf, Hussein Chalayan or Rodarte.

A good artistic director is someone who listens, offers good ideas, accepts guidelines and comes up with a solution that, without straying from the label philosophy, is fresh, original and alternative. Alexandre de Betak explained that his ultimate goal is to "make the show memorable, but you can't take away from the clothes. And you want to do something different and newsworthy, but you've got to stay within the image of the designer so people know where

they area."[2] Light and art director Thierry Dreyfus adds: "If the audience leaves the room saying how wonderful the light was, something has gone wrong. If the audience leaves excited about the music, again something has gone wrong. At end of the day what matters is the collection, and all elements must be used to reinforce its meaning and build brand identity."

According to Betak, it is vital to create a telegenic and photogenic event; as the pictures and videos will last long beyond the event. For this reason, when you begin to imagine a scenario, you do so in three dimensions, imagining the different angles of the magazine photographers, the television cameras and the label's own photographers.[3] The location of the audience is also fundamental as they will see the models show from the front row.

Nothing is left to chance, and that starts with the design of the runway itself. Art director Michael Brown lists the questions that arise every time you have to conceptualize the space for a runway: "What are the architectural and sculptural qualities of the location? Where is the entrance for guests? Where are they positioned to watch the runway show? How is the runway organized, sculpturally and graphically? What surface area does the runway cover and what will be the best option in combination with the clothes? Are the photographers located where they can take the best pictures? Where do models enter and exit?"

Constructing an evocative set that reproduces existing spaces or finding an actual remarkable location, such as a garage, terrace of a tall building, a gym or a park, is perhaps the greatest challenge.

Then, decisions on the lighting, music, the runway itself and the skin tone of the models will have to be made. In some cases, production companies use a few ideas as a starting point, and from here they take care of absolutely everything, while in others the company works along with them and helps to solve logistical problems.

Étienne Russo explains that in the case of Chanel, they take care of light, sound, technical direction and some elements of the set design. The other facets of the runway show (the decoration, the video production and the music played by runway shows DJ Michel Gaubert) are directly managed by Chanel. Each label has its own way of working and it is important to know when to delegate. The teams are flexible and are formed according to the requirements of the runway show. There are a certain number of permanent employees and a large number of potential collaborators, who can form teams of hundreds of people. Having a good creative, personal and effective art director is without a doubt one of the key elements to the success of the runway show. While there are many runway shows throughout fashion weeks, some of them stand out on their own. Michael Howells is the man behind all of John Galliano's spectacular productions. Moreover, Simon Costin, a dab hand at recreating magical and impossible scenarios in fashion shoots for magazines, is another regular.

His aim is to "dress" the space conceived by the artistic director. Parallel to the construction of space, the lighting of the event

TOP To celebrate the fiftieth runway show, Dries van Noten and Villa Eugénie staged a superb dinner for a select group of guests that ended with the presentation of the spring-summer 2005 collection on the table. © Photography by Patrice Stable, courtesy of Dries van Noten. **RIGHT** The classic runway has mutated into many forms. In the image, the curved runway by Tsumori Chisato with silk-screened words on the edges through which the models passed showing the spring-summer 2009 collection. © Photography by Mathias Wendzinski, courtesy of Eyesight.

has to be decided. The intangible and silent light, together with the music, helps to bring an air of excitement to the runway show. Exchanging views and graphic information is very useful to properly interpret the concept. Light defines an ambience, and it also highlights certain parts of the outfits, or it gives a satiny finish to the model's skin according to the idea that the designer has in mind. On other occasions, the designer, as was the case of Christian Lacroix, who produced his last runway show in summer 2009, and his company were responsible for the entire production of the runway show.

And while it is unusual for a fashion house to organize the entire production, it is usually the only option chosen by most young designers as it would not be feasi-

ble to hire large production companies. Henrik Vibskov is a good example of this. His spectacular runway shows, atypical and personal, always have a surprising production. To present his spring-summer 2008 collection, he devised the Fantabulous Bicycle Music Factory production, where the models, after showing the collection, got on a large machine designed for the occasion, forming part of an impressive choir-orchestra.

Defining the look: the stylist

Until recently, the stylists who are responsible mostly for the style and personality of a label had remained in the background, and only a few knew their names. The designers were the public face of the business, and stylists, as explained in the book that

Rizzoli has published recognizing their work, were "interpreters of fashion," who quietly and efficiently remained in the background to coherently put order to the collection according to current aesthetical standards. The most sought-after stylists usually charge about 4,000 euros a day, and work with the designer a few days before the runway show to define outfits and decide what types of accessories are suitable for the collection: shoes, handbags, jewelry, and even some pieces created specifically for the occasion. Katie Grand, stylist and current editor of *Love* magazine, and regularly contracted as a consultant for Louis Vuitton Menswear, Prada, and Miu Miu runway shows, said: "You'll have the whole design team there, and the creative di-

rector and the director of the whole company, all there watching you perform as you show your ideas."[4] It is important to work quickly and effectively: "When you're working with big designers and you've got a show next Sunday, you have to say: 'I like that, I don't like that, let's do that, let's do it in gray."[5] In every company there are work dynamics and different timings, so it is important that all the artistic team can adapt to the pace of its customers. "At Vuitton, it's very organized. You have the clothes six days before the show, and your job is a matter of putting them together and working with Marc [Jacobs] and their design team to make sure they like how it's put together. The process at Prada, on the other hand, is different. Miuccia Prada works in a particularly unique way where

the show evolves very late in the day,"[6] adds Katie Grand.

Carine Roitfeld, director of *Vogue Paris*, was a key component, in the words of experts, in the new sexy look of Gucci by Tom Ford. The fashion editor of the same magazine, Emmanuelle Alt, in recent seasons has given a new approach to the garments by French designer Isabel Marant. The designer explained that the stylist's work is crucial to lend a more sophisticated air to your clothing: "I am good at making clothes and dressing myself, but then dressing models, creating silhouettes... that's not my thing. I love it when she goes tac, tac, tac . . . puts the different pieces together, and I'm like: 'Oh, yeah! That's exactly it!' I don't think about the dressed girl like a lot of designers do. I'm interested in the separate pieces, but then I find it

hard to get them together again. Emmanuelle can take that step back. She has a clear and precise vision."[7]

British stylist Karl Templer has worked closely in recent years with Francisco Costa, designer for Calvin Klein, helping him with the fittings prior to the runway show. His work is not only to put together the outfits and choose the accessories, but rather, in Templer's own words, being "a second pair of eyes for the designer." And Francisco Costa himself points out: "He helps me to refine everything. The process feels very natural. We have really grown a lot together."[8]

The big designers usually present more than fifty outfits per runway show, but *Style.com* editor Laird Borrelli recommends to be concise and present, especially when starting out, between twenty-four

and thirty-six good, solid outfits. The order of presentation of the garments must make sense. Usually the more casual pieces are presented first to give way to the more sophisticated outfits. The more extravagant items are reserved to close the runway show. Just as some designers make use of some narrative to build their collection, it can be useful to have a common thread to present the pieces, fit the models, take pictures, put them next to each other and study closely to make sure the everything fits and forms a harmonious whole, compact and meaningful outfit, in order to be able to introduce changes of color and shape or to find the right accessories.

Miuccia Prada is a designer who builds the outfits as she goes and the night before a runway show she can make decisions that lead the collection to a whole new ball game. So the night before a runway show, Prada insisted on a change that clarified the whole collection: "I went there and [the hair] is too big and I say: 'Tie the hair.' By pulling it aside, everything became German. It was so obvious. This is the interesting part. You do it and with a little change you see the whole thing differently."[9] Hair styles and make up are part of the outfit, and for this reason during the fittings, make up and hair trials are also carried out. The same collection can be interpreted in many different ways. Finding the right interpretation requires experience and a vision that connects with the public and helps build brand identity.

New faces: the casting director

Although presentations of collections without models do exist, they add the human element to the spectacular and technological productions. Slim, slender and beautiful, their faces reproduce rapidly and often are one of main attractions for the media. Today, many labels are still hiring the top-models from the eighties as an added extra for their fashion shows as with them on the runway, the non-stop camera flashes are a sure bet.

A casting director is in charge of choosing the models. The casting director is an independent professional who works directly for both labels and is subcontracted by production agencies. He also works as a middle man between various agencies and the designer. Choosing models with a certain criteria or a certain style in mind can be a determining factor for the success of a consistent

runway show. The Hedi Slimane castings for Dior Homme are a good example of this, as many of the boys were headhunted in the street. Their unusual faces and frail bodies that seemed to be custom-made to wear his clothes became one of its hallmarks.

Depending on your budget and designer's image of the girl or boy, the casting director will search for those faces and bodies that will act as ambassadors for the clothes in front of the media and who will attend a casting that normally opens a few weeks before the show. The most sought-after models are directly chosen, in what is called a direct booking. The others, who are in the city or come to it expressly for the casting, have to show their book, informally pose for some snapshots, try on some clothes and walk to check that they move correctly. The agencies send the models to the casting who in their opinion best fit the designer's profile.

Some casting directors such as Russell Marsh or James Scully are experts in designing teams of models based on the label's requirements. Marsh, who can test some one hundred images per day and have a look at three thounsand models per year and who has a database of over eighteen thousand models from all over the world, has been doing castings for over ten years for Prada.[10] After consulting and scanning the proposals from the best agencies, he holds a casting for one hundred and fifty girls, of whom he selects fifteen or twenty per runway show. Models Daria Webowy (face of Chanel, Dior, Balmain, Prada, Vuitton and Cavalli, to name a few) and Gemma Ward, discovered on the Sydney runway (the face of Prada, Dior and Dolce & Gabbana) were both discovered by Marsh.

LEFT Top model Chanel Iman poses in a dress from the spring-summer collection of designer Frankie Morello. © Photography by Sonny Vandevelde. **RIGHT** The casting director for the 2009 Bruno Pieters spring-summer show peruses a model's portfolio. © Fotography by Sonny Vandevelde.

Casting director James Scully worked closely choosing girls for Tom Ford, both for Gucci and YSL runway shows, and has also worked regularly creating castings for Stella McCartney, Carolina Herrera and Zac Posen's fashion shows. For each designer he configures a different group, and while in the casting process Scully tells a *Nymag.com*[11] journalist that for Carolina Herrera he looks for "girls with richness and poise, and a bit of the Park Avenue matron in them," while for the Derek Lam casting he chooses girls who are "lighter, sexier and more sensual." Expe-

rience forces casting directors to make quick decisions: with just one look they can tell whether or not a rough diamond is standing in front of them. The percentage of new faces among those chosen depends greatly on the designer, while some prefer to work with models that the public can easily recognize, others prefer to take a risk and use new faces.

The designer often chooses their favorite models to open and close the runway show. These models are sure to be the ones who do more campaigns or who will pose for more front covers the following season: those who

have opened or closed more runway shows are those who will gain more popularity. The group of models selected to show for a particular label is called the *cabine*, a term that comes from the group of models that the top houses hired during long trial sessions prior to the show.

For an unknown face, opening the show can be quite an honor, but it is not necessary to open the show to achieve notoriety. To be chosen out of fifty models in a casting for a big designer can be the launch of a career. Also, fashion magazines often devote spaces to these new faces each season, contributing to this "discovery" phenomenon. The American model Hilary Rhoda, who currently has an exclusive contract with Estée Lauder, caught the attention of the Balenciaga designer Nicolas Ghesquière in runway shows in New York. He then chose her to model in Paris and in turn introduced her to his friend Aerin Lauder, the creative director of the cosmetics firm.

From the front row, publishers and customers search for new faces, and minutes before the show there is great anticipation to see which models have been chosen. "It was great because we are always looking for new girls, and all the new girls of New York were on the runway, so it was a good idea for casting, very fresh and suitable with these clothes,"[12] adds Carine Roitfeld, director of *Vogue Paris* when the Marc by Marc Jacobs show finished. Designer Marc Jacobs usually presents a casting with a large number of new fresh and natural faces for the runway show of his second line, Marc by Marc Jacobs. The journalist Harriet Quick closes her book *Catwalking*[13] with the instructions that the designer gave in his 1996 runway show to the models: "Boys and girls. Please walk at a natural pace, not slow, not fast. Please, no hands on hips. No turns. No modeling! Thank you. You are all beautiful and we love you."

The instructions are written on a large card that hangs in a visible place backstage and provides guidelines for the models to easily adapt to the character that matches the set, hairstyle, make up, music and ultimately, with the message that the house wants to convey. Known as cue cards or moodboards, they are very useful, especially for those models who come directly from another runway show (some may model

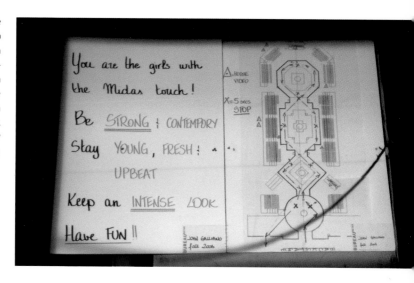

in more than six runway shows), and they need to get into the role quickly.

The cue cards that Alexandre de Betak prepares for his shows are worth keeping; they are synthetic and fun and are remembered fondly by many models.[14] These cards are also accompanied by diagrams in which the producer draws clearly the exit point, the path and the entry point that the models must follow. The choreography of the models on the runway needs to be thoroughly studied and can be developed in many different ways. The opening and closing of the runway show are the highlights, and are often the most intense moments. But every movement must be imagined to coordinate all the elements that act in the production: the lighting, music and the special effects. In the more tradi-tional formats, experiments and surprises are normally reserved for the beginning and end of the runway show, while in the middle of the presentation the outfits are more synthetic involving the models moving on the circuit and stopping where necessary. The models stop where the photogra-phers and television cameras can view them best, so that they can take a clear image. In the end, all models come out again and greet the attendees along with the de-signer.

Interestingly, the prototype of runway models has been molded over time. Now most design-ers choose very tall, thin models with personal and unusual faces. The distance between the idyl-lic model on the runway and the public has gradually grown in re-cent years. This gap has caused a bitter argument about the im-pact that these ideas of beauty may have on a society that in-creasingly seeks to be like these bodies that represent the idea of perfection. In an unprecedented move, the Cibeles de Madrid Runway from 2006 has imposed a minimum BMI for participat-ing models. While other fashion weeks have not joined this initia-tive, it has resulted in new regula-tions being introduced, such as banning models under sixteen and forcing the model to present a medical certificate guaranteeing their good health.

Eugene Souleiman

Stylist
www.streeterslondon.com

Eugene Souleiman is one of the most influential hair stylists in the world of fashion, a true visionary who creates trends that are followed by stylists, makeup artists and hairdressers. His outgoing and good-humoured personality has helped to create hairstyles that have left their mark. In 1997 he made his debut as a hair stylist in the Hussein Chalayan runway show and since then his phone has not stopped ringing. Accompanied by his team, Eugene works under pressure in the long list of runway shows that fill his busy schedule: Chanel, Dries van Noten, Ann Demeulemeester, Donna Karan, Louis Vuitton, Narciso Rodriguez, Moschino, Viktor & Rolf, etc.

In each runway show you work with your own professional team, how many people are in the team?

My team consists of fifteen people; we have been working together for many years, so you could say we are like one big family. We spend a lot of time together, sometimes, if the hairstyles are quite complicated, we spend days practising before the runway show. My best friend, Martin Cullen, is a freelance hair stylist he manages the rest of the team. He coordinates fitting times of the runway shows . . . He ensures that everything is ready at the right time, in short, he organizes almost everything, which leaves

stress. How would you describe the atmosphere?

The backstage atmosphere varies from one designer to another. Each label has a philosophy and a different way of functioning and the designer's personality also is a factor. There is not one backstage the same as another. One of the things I like about my job, is that one runway show is never the same as another, I'm never bored. The star models usually arrive about forty-five minutes before the runway show, which makes it quite hard work because you only have about ten or fifteen minutes to do their hair and there are times

For the fall-winter 2009 runway show by Tsumori Chisato, Eugene created an intricate braid. © Photography by Matthew Lever.

> *"To be visionary you have to believe in your own ideas and not be afraid to take risks"*

me enough time and energy to think about new ideas. I like working at a fast pace and under pressure. I think it brings the best out of my team and me.

When we see backstage pictures of runway shows in magazines they always convey a sense of ongoing

you have to undo her hair, wash it and start again. There are models that arrive about ten minutes before a runway show, so you have to do their make up and hair in a short time. Working against the clock is the most stressful and exhausting thing about my work.

Model Lena Lomkova wears her hair style inspired by the athletes in motion, reinforcing the concept of Inertia collection spring-summer 2009 by Hussein Chalayan.

Having worked in over thirty runway shows, tell us what has been the most stressful time in your career?
It was one runway show in Paris, crazy! All the models appeared half an hour before the runway show and we had to do the hair and make up of thirty-five girls in just fifteen minutes. And the craziest? The last Alexander McQueen for Givenchy runway show. The whole team was working on two wigs for two days and two nights before the runway show. We prepared every last detail, and as it was the last col-

when we are all most tired, yet, we work hard to make it the best of all runway shows.

How much time do you spend creating ideas for a runway show?
It depends on the designer. Some just want to talk to you over the phone, send emails and photos for inspiration. But the best thing is to see the collection, go along to the fitting for the models and listen to music that will be played on the runway: it is a magic aura that you inevitably join and take part

For spring-summer 2009 collection by designer Yohji Yamamoto, Eugene and his team created some ethereal hairstyles.

"*A parade is fifteen minutes walk of beautiful women with incredible clothes to the strains of fantastic music*"

lection McQueen would design for Givenchy we thought backstage would be full of press and we wanted everything to be perfect. Before the runway show we found out that he had not invited anyone backstage and we'd be alone with the models and team. At that moment we all burst out

in to strengthen the designer's original idea. I love working with runway shows because you help realize the vision of the designer and you only have one chance to make it perfect. For a label the runway show is very important, not only as a presentation of the collection, but as a

Which model is easiest to work with?

Raquel Zimmermann. She is fun, she's like an actress, she understands the clothes on the runway, the photographs and she enjoys seeing herself with different styles, she can play the role of being young and foolish, childish, romantic or simply sexy.

In your opinion what is a runway show?

Fifteen minutes of beautiful women walking down the runway with stunning outfits and great music.

Are you worried about the opinions of those sitting in the front row?

To be honest, no. I am quite a strong person. What really matters is creating an opinion, whether it is good or bad. The best compliment you can receive from a fashion editor is: it is the best hairstyle I've ever seen! In contrast, a bad review makes me stronger and I try to surpass myself. I think to be a visionary you have to have a voice, take risks without being afraid of making mistakes and having the strength to rise again and start again if things don't go well.

Can you give advice to emerging makeup artists and hair stylists?

Always listen to the designer and stylist to create a unique vision that fits in with the concept that the designer wants to convey. Never think that the hair stylist's role is isolated, you should keep in mind that a runway show is the sum of the teamwork of several professionals.

Eugene and one of his assitants in the creative throes backstage at Tsumori Chisato. © Photography by Matthew

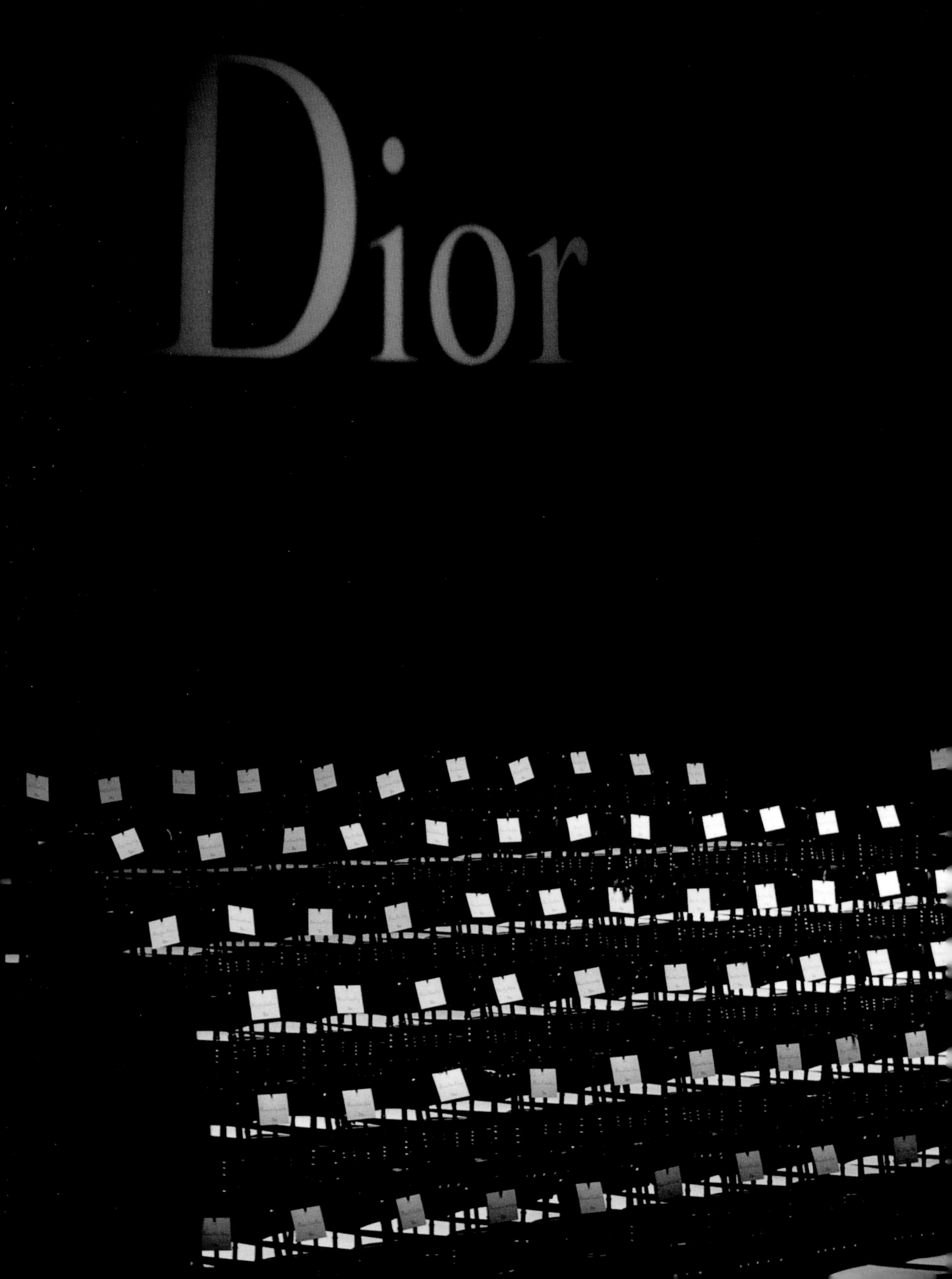
Dior

Diffusion

A small purple enveloped has arrived at the office. It reads your name in gold letters and the name of an unfamiliar designer. You open it and a wonderful little display of paper unfolds before your eyes, you reread the name and type into Google. His website, simple, clear and professional, shows you a small preview of what the first collection will be. These romantic-inspired dresses may fit with the style of the magazine, an independent publication that has managed to break into the complicated world of publishing. You write it down in your agenda, you do not want to miss how it all begins.

Backstage at the Dior haute couture spring-summer 2009 runway show.© Photography by David Ramos.

Press office

The press or public relations office manages all the communication needs that a fashion label may require. It works on and creates communication strategies to publicize the label and it provides graphic and written information to the media when required. Some designers outsource communication agencies and benefit from the synergies and contacts that these agencies already have. Others prefer to handle issues associated with the media in-house, and for this they have a small team of professionals. The economic factor, again, plays a major role in this factor, as the services of a press agency cost at least 1,200 euros per month.

Newcomers will more than likely take charge of the public relations work and maybe contract someone twice a year to ensure the presence of the press at their runway shows.

It is important that the press office works alongside the designer and the production team. The press office, when it has gathered all the required information, would have to prepare the guest list, order invitations, send a note with detailed information of the event, provide all facilities to the media, schedule interviews, hire a photographer to take pictures for label, meet the models who will take part in the show and the group that will perform live etc. The basic objective is to inform and create news, so that the event is made public and attracts the attention of the media.

The communication plan

The presentation of the collection is a powerful communication element that has an important role in the label's communication plan. Knowing who the target audience is will help to choose the location, to decide the best way to do it and establish the guest

LEFT At the entrance of the haute couture spring-summer 2009 by Jean Paul Gaultier, a familiar face attracts the attentions of the flashes and the press. © Photography by David Ramos. **TOP** A journalist takes notes in the specially-made brochure for the Christian Lacroix 2009 spring haute couture show. © Photography by David Ramos.

list. By choosing one format or another, one model or another, will define the type of media that will be interested in publishing our material and, ultimately, the public to whom we will present the collection.

In order to determine with which publications to work, the style of the magazine, its frequency, distribution and its readership should be considered. It will be necessary to do some field work, get to know and enter contacts into the database of journalists from publications that the collection would be compatible with, whether it is a summary of the runway show or a photo collage during the after-party or just so the editors would consider the label as a proposal to be considered for future editions. *Love*, *Vogue* and *Nylon* have very different target audiences, and

you must discern which of them you want to make contact with. Attracting the more institution-alized media attention is something that can be complicated and frustrating for a newcomer, so it is advisable to start with more affordable alternatives. Online publications are a good option to generate news, they tend to focus on smaller brands if the material is good. *Hint Fashion Magazine*, *Refinery 29* or *Style Bubble* are on-line publications that place special emphasis on new designers and are consulted diligently by editors, stylists and professionals of the big publications.[1]

Luck, good contacts, charisma, offering an innovative and commercial product, but above all, satisfying current needs and good presentation are some of the compulsory characteristics. There are

many variables and is not easy to find the correct formula. Christopher Kane played his cards masterly in his debut. The fashion editor Stephen Doig began the review of his first show as follows: "There are certain moments in fashion history where you want to be able to say: 'I was there.'"[2]

Sponsored by NewGen, Kane drew the attention of Anna Wintour in a review on promising fashion students, which appeared in *Vogue*; after the show they all wore their tight dresses. Not much later, Donatella Versace hired him as an assistant and then came his collection for Topshop. An irony of life, Kane's vocation for fashion was awakened when he saw John Galliano's graduation runway show on the BBC.

But his case is one in a million. Only a lucky few of the many tal-

LEFT Ivana Trump, on the left, is seated in the front row sitting next to other celebrities at the start of haute couture Christian Lacroix runway show. © Photography by David Ramos. TOP In the front row, waiting for the fall-winter 2009 runway show by Bernhard Willhelm to begin. © Photography by Daniel Mayer.

ented and skilled students that leave the schools rise to fame so fast. Simon Doonan, the Barneys store director in New York, made a bitter reflection: "The fashion system is doing a terrible disservice to students and young designers by making them think they can become the next Tom Ford by putting on a great fashion show."[3] On the other side of the coin are those who dream of someday seeing their clothes on the cover of *Vogue*, there are designers who are very aware of their resources and capabilities, and who are comfortable operating in the background, with small but solvent companies that develop slowly and steadily. In short, it is about knowing how to present your collection and from where. The independent designer Bernhard Willhelm, with his experi-

ence of quite a few runway shows, discusses how to address this issue: "In the beginning, you want to play by the rules. You want to be in those magazines but, in the end, they ignore you or you realise this is not what you want. In the end, I was like: 'Who cares?' [. . .]. So now we just do what we feel like doing. We also started doing films and installations because it's another freedom."[4]

The guest list

Preparing the guest list is not easy. The first thing is to know the capacity of the space holding the show to determine the number of people you can invite. It is also important to update the database.

Regarding the guests, you will have to consider several different groups to put together a bal-

LEFT From the front row, the audience contemplates in detail the haute couture proposal by the designer Christian Lacroix for spring 2009 which the model Niari Aminata wears. © Photography by David Ramos. RIGHT Applause at the end of the fall-winter 2009 runway show by Bernhard Willhelm. © Photography by Daniel Mayer.

anced, representative list, which leaves no one out: the press, VIPs, photographers, buyers, customers. If the runway show is within the context of an institutionalized fashion week, it is likely that the organization will provide in advance a document with the media that have requested accreditation. Among the press, there is a distinction between international and national press, offline and online, printed and graphic media and backstage photographers and the television cameras and reporters. On paper, the designer decides along with the press of-

fice who they should invite and who they shouldn't.

The accreditation is a badge that bears the name of the journalist and where he/she works. This must be requested from the organization of the runway show several weeks in advance and it serves as ID for security and members of protocol who flank the entrance and ensures no-hassle entry.

The other guests include publishers, editors, buyers and end customers known by the label, VIPs and media personalities who often attract media attention. All the guests preferably have been sent a hand-written

personalized invitation, as it always gives the invitation a more personal touch, and if you have a close relationship with the guest, attach a short note.

Many designers invest a significant portion of their budget on creating a top-quality colorful and surprising invitation, which will create anticipation among the guests about what they will see on the day. The invitation should suggest the character of the collection and the mood of the runway show, prompting imagination, remembrance and the generation of excitement. These graphic pieces will be one

of the few lasting reminders after the big day, and many fashion editors, students and fans of the label will keep it as a small keepsake.

Many fashion houses regularly work with the same art director. This develops the brand identity along with its philosophy, defining the visual language of the campaigns, coordinating photo shoots, developing the lookbooks, the catalogue, etc. The invitation may be accompanied by a small gadget or gift intended for a select group on the guest list.

A cute flip book that gives life to smiling lips was the format that Maison Martin Margiela chose for the invitation of its menswear spring-summer 2001 collection. At Dior Homme minimalism is imposed on a sober and elegant invitation: a white placard with black print and a minimum font, just enough information to get there, in an envelope, printed through a hole, the title of the collection in big bold letters: "Cold Love." John Galliano drew inspiration from old postcards, and he made his own version of decorating the piece with aesthetics associated with the house. At Prada, as a preview to what guests were later going to see projected on the walls of the location, a typographical game made from snippets of conversations among the male stars. Labels usually follow a global line, which gives coherence to their image, and for this reason, the invitations have certain common elements between seasons so that when the person receiving the envelope opens it, they can easily recognize the sender. According to the corporate identity the formats of

TOP Gift for guests at the spring-summer 2009 runway show by Tsumori Chisato in Paris. © Photography by Mathias Wendzinski, courtesy of Eyesight. **RIGHT** The stewards, in position, attend to the first guests in the haute couture show by Christian Lacroix. © Photography by David Ramos.

the envelopes, paper and printing are chosen.

The invitation must be creative, true to the spirit of the label and have a professional finish. The help of a graphic designer is advisable. It is important not to forget any details; once they are printed there is no turning back. Be sure to provide the basic information about when, where and what. A press contact and a phone number to confirm attendance are also essential.

The use of a single ink, screen printing, stamps, or more economical paper can help cut costs. For some, the choice of the suitable invitation comes down to something much more simple: "When I design the invitation for one of my fashion shows, I will write Suzy's name on the trial proof. If her name looks good on it, I know I can send it" says the designer Alber Elbaz, the head at Lanvin.[5]

For big labels like Lanvin, it is a good idea to hold a press conference as all the media wants to be there. The tricky part is when you have to decide who to leave out. For newcomers, however, attracting press attention and securing the guests is an adventure in itself. Normally, some 70% of invitations that have been sent can be disregarded. Out of the 30% who respond, approximately one-third may not appear. Deciding the location of the show can be decisive, although sometimes you do not know which is better, to do do it on the same day as the big names and take in the stragglers, or find a day that does not compete with other events. Once you have sent out the invitations, it is advisable to follow up, call the guests who you really want to attend to remind them about the event and to be able to make an estimate of the number of people who will attend the runway show. Similar to the guest list, make a list of the media and people communicating the celebration of the event with a small press release about the presentation. The list should be effective to get the message across to those who might be interested. Publishers receive hundreds of press releases each week and often have no time to deal with them.

The seating plan

The seating plan refers to the distribution of seats in the runway shows. The seating plan is prepared from the list of confirmed guests and its preparation requires

great diplomatic skill. The front rows are reserved for the most influential journalists, the best buyers and celebrities at the runway shows of all the big names.

In runway shows in Paris, the seating is clearly defined and arranged in order of importance. On both sides of the runway there are separate blocks for VIPs and magazine publishers and editors and buyers. The French journalists have their own area, the Americans and British with another area, Japan and Italy share an area and the rest of Europe is located behind the television cameras. The journalists of publications with greater media coverage get the best positions. Mark Tungate reveals: "Fashion journalists will tell you that it is vital that they sit in the front row, because it enables them to see the clothes properly—including the shoes. But, off the record, they admit that it is as much about status as it is about professionalism."[6]

The press office should make name places for those people who must be seated in a privileged location. These cards will be placed on the chairs to avoid confusion. Generic cards are also made denoting areas reserved exclusively for press, VIPs or guests.

Careful coordination among all team members is vital, as is updating the guest list and relocating positions right up to the last minute, so that, when the runway show begins, everyone is in place. There is one person responsible for seating in the press office. Their main function is to be aware of the relationships between different guests: what positions they hold, who gets on well with whom, direct competitors in the media. This information is important to avoid any uneasy and uncomfortable situations.

Today many bloggers, followed daily by thousands of Internet

Dior

LEFT A guest at the Christian Dior runway show holds the press dossier in his arms. © Photography by Gerard Estadella. **RIGHT** Mónica, from the blog Miss at la Playa, took this snapshot of Masha Novoselov backstage at the Cibeles de Madrid runway show to publicize her blog.

users, have become mini celebrities. Through their pages, they generate waves of opinion and it is important to keep up-to-date to detect these new profiles to be included in the lists. Some designers have taken note and the specialized press, such as *WWD* has echoed this phenomenon: "Bloggers are now officially front row material." Well, this was surely the case in the Dolce & Gabbana runway show where bloggers Brian Boy, Tommy Ton, Scott Schuman and Garance Doré were seated in the front row next to Anna Wintour and Suzy Menkes.

Press dossier

Besides the invitation the press dossier must be prepared, a folder that is handed out to guests and which usually includes a press release on the collection and a CD or USB with the graphic material so that journalists have additional information apart from just the notes taken during the runway show. The clear and simple press release should be no longer than one page and should have the following structure: a title which includes the season and the title of the collection, a first paragraph that summarizes synthetically the contents of the note and a text ex-

plaining point by point features of the collection such as the inspiration, the fabrics used and the type of client that it is aimed at. The fashion editor Sarah Cristobal from *Stylelist* comments: "The press release is a reflection of the product to be sold. It must be carefully designed and reviewed to ensure there are no typos or errors. It is important that the press releases are consistent and flawless."

Picture material

Having a good photographer to document the event is a basic requirement. These images can

offer material to the press and buyers, drawing up the book and building our website. You need to hire a photographer specializing in runway shows who can take clear, good quality pictures. It is vital to give the photographer the precise instructions of what you need: full shots, close-ups focusing on the details of the fabrics or accessories or general full shots of the production. The better the quality of these images, the more coverage they will get in the press.

Personal interviews

The press will want to interview the designer before or after the show to get firsthand information about the collection. Public relations should coordinate these meetings, which have a mutual benefit for both parties. The designer, on the day of the runway show, will be very busy and can only devote a small portion of their time to the press, selectivity is the key.

New means of communication

Besides the traditional means of issuing the press release, the use of social networks, such as Facebook or Twitter, are increasingly common, thereby multiplying the communication links. If the mailing list is normally managed from the press office unilaterally, now the users themselves can subscribe to the newsletter on the webpage, deciding what information they regularly want to receive on the label. This is a new factor that reflects the changes in relationships between the company and its potential end customers.

© Greg Kessler

Sonny Vandevelde

Photographer
www.sonnyphotos.typepad.com

Raised in Australia, Vandevelde covers the fashion capitals with camera in hand to show the ins and outs of the runway shows of your favorite designers, whether they are big names or small independent designers. Dynamic and a fashion enthusiast, he is the perfect accomplice, managing to get big smiles from all the most beautiful models wherever he goes. We can appreciate his spontaneous photos of the leading collections from the other side. Apart from working on his personal blog, he collaborates with the online magazine online *Hint Fashion Magazine*, which, season after season, publishes a selection of his work, and with the blog of the journalist Diane Pernet.

What is a backstage photographer?
The backstage photographer remains in the back to show the preparation, glamour, fun and hard work behind a runway show. Although for me, mainly, it's about showing the fun side.

How did it all begin?
As a fashion photographer, it began when I was invited to a runway show and I could not wait for it to begin to see the girls, some of which I know, walking down the runway all somber and solemn. So I ran backstage and took pictures to kill time. Some publishers liked the result and asked me to do more.

It seems that you really enjoy your work.
Well, first of all and I would like to make this clear, I do not earn much money from it. It is more like a hobby. I love fashion, and to be immersed in a space with the best makeup artists, the best hairdressers, the best stylists and the best models with latest collection seems a bit surreal to me! After having spent many years backstage, on the way to the first show of the season I still have butterflies in my stomach and I'm really excited.

Do you remember the most stressful backstage situation than you've

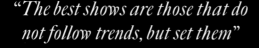

> "*The best shows are those that do not follow trends, but set them*"

What do you like to take photos of backstage?
I want fun and crazy photos, those in which the models let down their guard for a second. I also like the action shots; you know when they are in a hurry to change.

ever photographed?
The stressful moments are those when public relations are really stressed . . . But there is no need for it, because it just infects the rest of the team. I hate stress, I hate the word. It is not even a real word, it is an invention of the nineties! I prefer

Backstage details taken by Sonny. **TOP** Tao Okamoto, Zina Zinovenkova, and the diseñador Alexandre Herchcovitch in the background, during the final moments before their 2009 fall-winter show. © Photography by Sonny Vandevelde. **BOTTOM** The models mess around before the Bernhard Willhelm runway show. ON THE **FOLLOWING PAGE** Kinga Rajzak and Daul Kim at the Rodarte runway show.

words like overworked, tired, hands full, without a minute of spare time . . . Curiously, the best runway shows are those of veteran designers, who have had many successful shows. Minutes before starting they are relaxed, and ready to go.

And the craziest?
Crazy, in the best sense of the word, those of John Galliano. There is always so much emotion, so much creativity and power in the shows . . . I live for them.

Is it possible to feel the success of a collection backstage?
Yes, but I don't focus on that when I arrive. I try to focus on who the models are, I look at the lighting and decor, imagining how photos will turn out. It is when I see the girls lined up ready to go with their outfits when I pay attention to all the clothes and I choose my favorite outfit. Very rarely have I left backstage without taking my camera. It has happened, but rarely. I even think in the worst collection you can salvage something fantastic.

What kind of runway show do you find most interesting?
Those that are not aimed at a mass market, those which show a vision, an original idea, that do not follow trends, they set trends. And also those which cast good models.

New York, Paris, London and Milan are the big four. What do you like most about each of the cities?
Paris stands out from any other destination, as it has it all: the luxurious fashion houses, the leading labels and the small firms and emerging talent. New York is the most commercial city and where the celebrities flock to. And, to be honest, I do not really like it when the shows are taken over by celebrities. In some runway shows, and this happens in Berlin too, it seems that celebrities are the focus of the event. And it should not be this way. The best bit about New York is that you can eat anytime and anywhere, there you will find good and healthy food late at night after the show, when there is still a lot of work to do, something which in Paris is difficult. Apart from the big four, I have had good experiences in Stockholm and I would like to go to Denmark someday. And of course, Sydney is always marked on my calendar.

In your opinion, what does a runway show need to stand out?
Originality, good music, the best makeup and hair artists that money can find, a talented casting agent to select the best models . . . and me, of course, to document backstage.

KAMILA

The big day

Six months of exhaustive work concentrated into a brief exhibition in which the shameless, curious, defiant, indifferent, playful and critical glances understand, measure and compare the collection. The big day has arrived and the most important details are already decided. Now all that is needed is to supervise, help and let nature take its course. Fifteen minutes and it's over. They applaud, oh yes, they applaud. It seems that they liked it. You go out onto the runway and greet the crowds. On your way back, your eye catches a lady in the front row who is wearing a showy hat. Next season, hats and lots of them, you think to yourself. And it all begins again.

Naomi Campbell models in a beautiful Wild West inspired set designed by Villa Eugénie designed for spring-summer 2009 runway show by Hermès. © Photography by By2photographers, courtesy of Villa Eugénie.

Building anticipation

Today is the day of the runway show. A few days before a short note has been sent to the press with a sneak preview of what they can expect. Who will model, what types of garments will be presented or which group will put the soundtrack to the event: these elements can be the just the thing to create expectation and attract those who are undecided.

From early morning, the art director will give the technical team indications on where they have to work, while they draw a sketch of the runway floor with instructions for the models on a large piece of card. The technicians, as fast as possible, start to put the lights and spotlights in place, while the lighting director carries out the first tests. Photometer in hand he/she measures the temperatures and the color with the suitable light.

Backstage

From early morning, this is one of the busiest spaces. First, it has to be prepared for the hair and makeup artists, models and stylists to work comfortably and with the proper lighting. Like a small army, they arrive loaded with luggage.

The makeup artist Pat McGrath, the person behind the exotic and colorful makeup for Prada, Miu Miu and Comme des Garcons, has been known to arrive with more than sixty suitcases full of material. In a few days, after studying the collection, the makeup artist has decided along with the designer what makeup will be used for the runway show. When the feedback has been received, the trials begin in order to achieve the desired result. For most runway shows, two different looks are created; however

RIGHT White is the hallmark of the Maison Martin Margiela, and this was the scenario devised by Villa Eugénie for the spring-summer 2007 runway show of the label. © Photography by By2photographers, courtesy of Villa Eugénie. **TOP** © Photography by Clive Booth.

LEFT Above, a model reads while having her hair done backstage at Dior. © Photography by David Ramos. Bottom, the hairdresser works on a hairstyle for the spring-summer 2009 couture runway show by Jean Paul Gaultier. © Photography by David Ramos. RIGHT Two dressers puts the final touches to the dress that Romina Lanaro will wear for the fall-winter runway show by Hussein Chalayan. © Photography by Sonny Vandenvelde.

on some occasions working with the designer is more thorough. For John Galliano, Pat McGrath creates a lot of makeup styles that are tested several times. Then, the material is sent to the designer, who approves it along with some pointers. As stated in *Time* magazine, "every designer takes you on a different journey. It's great when they let you into their fantasy."[1] The models are called about four hours before the runway show,

ON THIS PAGE. Some of the pages of the *Backstage Magazine* which is available online at www.backstage-mag.com, with art direction and photography by Christina Mayer and Daniel Mayer. Clockwise and starting from top right: three pictures from the Bernhard Willhelm runway show, cover of the Bless No.31 runway show, cover of the Tsumori Chisato runway show, a double page in the interior and in the centre, Pamela Anderson on the cover of the Vivienne Westwood fall-winter 2009 runway show. © Photography by Daniel Mayer.

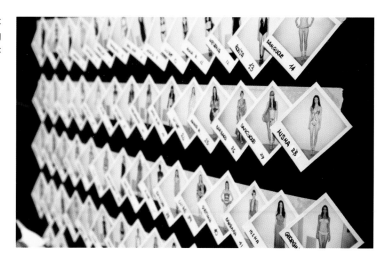

but everything depends on the complexity of the makeup, hair and clothing. The trials and fittings carried out the previous days help to plan the time required for each of the processes involved in a runway show. Hairdressers and makeup artists should be coordinated to prepare the twenty to thirty models in the shortest space of time possible.

While the combs and brushes work at the speed of light, the dressers unpack the clothes, iron them, carry out the final touches and hang them on rails, normally one per model. A piece of card attached to the rail bears the models name with full body photographs, Polaroid or digital, of each of the outfits that she will wear. These also include explanations and even photographs of the accessories for the outfit: earrings, bags, tights and shoes.

One or two people are required to dress the model and to make quick and effective changes.

Amid the frenetic activity, an essential person moves to capture the unique moments typical of the world of fashion. This person is the backstage photographer. Greg Kessler does not miss an opportunity, and since he was fifteen he has photographed collections in their natural surroundings. He is fascinated by the "transformation and the circus" and said: "There are so many great and talented people working on each show all jammed into one space for the sole purpose of making what the audience and fashion world see so beautiful. It's really a roller coaster."[2] Months later, his images are used in the special biannual supplements of the fashion magazines dedicated to runway shows. *Style.com*, *The New York Times*, *Number* or *Elle* regularly publishes his work. Amid so much movement, backstage photographers help calm nerves, making the long wait pass as quickly as possible.

Sonny Vandevelde manages to create a very special complicity with the models who he portrays: nerves, excitement, hope, stress are emotions that he accurately captures. Sonny, with no fixed abode, not only covers the largest runway shows, but also presentations by lesser known designers. His pictures are assiduously used to illustrate the blog of personal fashion journalist Diane Pernet. A reality that dramatically contrasts with the other side of the coin. Out on the runway, things move at a different pace.

Daniel and Christina Mayer, the former is a photographer specializing in portraits and the latter is

a graphic designer, have created online *Backstage Magazine*, which compiles everything that happens backstage minutes before the runway show of designers such as Tsumori Chisato, Bless, Valentino and Vivienne Westwood. This creative combo can take beautiful portraits in an area, which is generally quite difficult to take good portraits, "the backstage; it is a very intense intimate time in which the team tries to give their best."

The trial run

A couple of hours after backstage gives the go-ahead for the show to begin, it pauses for one of the most crucial moments of the day: the trial run. This is when we find out if the production runs like clockwork: the order of appearance of the outfits, the choreography of the models, the play of

lights and music have to be perfectly coordinated. This is a good time to give the models advice, although they are only half ready, they may decide to wear heels to more realistically recreate the situation that will take place a few hours later. The models must time their walks with the music, vital for a smooth choreography. Normally, there is one trial run on the same day or the day before, however some designers prefer to do more than one. John Galliano, three days before the event has the choreography perfected, or the Japanese Rei Kawakubo, designer of Comme des Garçons, Issey Miyake or Yohji Yamamoto, can hold three trial runs for each runway show.[3]

The line-up

When the trial runs are over, which usually last between thirty

and sixty minutes, backstage the frenetic activity resumes. Half an hour before the show, the models are dressed in the first outfit that they will wear by the team of dressers, who carry out the finishing touches. The designer checks that the instructions have been followed correctly and checks that everything is perfect: make-up, hair, accessories, etc. Making sure everything looks just as he/she had imagined. The models are lined up according to the order of appearance and the stage manager reminds them of some of the key aspects of the choreography.

The photographers

Away from the bustle of backstage, and in their special reserved area, the runway photographers take their positions hours before the start of the

LEFT Measuring the light with a photometer moments before the haute couture spring-summer 2009 runway show by Elie Saab. © Photography by David Ramos. **RIGHT** The photographers' marks clearly limit their space during the Paris haute couture week. Seniority, experience and perseverance can be determining factors in being chosen to model first in the runway show. © Photography by David Ramos.

runway show. With colored tape, they mark their floor space, and the assistant keeps a lookout so that a few minutes before the runway show the photographer arrives and takes his/her position. Unmentioned in most articles, they are the real stars of the evening and their testimony transfers the magic of the fashion shows to the most popular magazines. The producer Alexandre de Betak believes the position of the photographers is fundamental when designing the runway show space, by determining the position of the photographers, he is deciding and marking the image that later will be reproduced in the media: "My goal is to create photogenic events. This is the purpose of set designing: to ensure that the label receives as much media coverage as possible."[4] In the early days when runway shows were a communication tool, photos were vetoed for fear of imitations. Only written memories are preserved of the extravagant and careful productions of runway shows by the designer Elsa Schiaparelli in the thirties because photographers were not allowed to attend her presentations. The role of photographers in runway shows has been unsettled and complex, and some labels have consequently regulated the conditions and the use of the images depending on label's business and media interests at that time.[5]

There are photographers who specialize in capturing the exact commercial image, taking shots at passing models: close-ups, back shots and detailed shots to cover all angles. A few agencies control the majority of images in the runway shows. The agency Zeppelin, founded by Marcio Madeira, with offices in Paris and New York, regularly collaborates with *Style.com* and has its own online website selling photographs, FirstView.com, the self-proclaimed "world's largest database and photographic archive, with 2,837,903 fashion photography, videos and much more."

Maria Valentino, FirstView contributor, explains that taking a photograph on the runway is not as easy as it looks: "It requires much physical stamina and concentration for short periods. A typical fashion show only lasts about fifteen minutes, but working for long hours, sometimes often twelve to sixteen hour days. Almost any photographer can shoot one fashion show well. But shooting fifty of them in a row well is quite another story."[6]

LEFT A photographer discovers, once the runway show has finished, the result of her shots. © Photography by David Ramos. RIGHT Images of the opening by Charlotte di Calypso's haute couture spring 2009 runway show by John Galliano for Dior. © Photography by David Ramos.

The front row

Sitting in the front row is a privilege exclusively reserved for the most prestigious publishers, publications managers, VIPs and department store buyers. Minutes before the runway show commences, the guests offer an alternative show in the entrance to the building where the collection is presented. Wearing their Sunday best, they wait patiently for the doors of the building to open. Photographer Tommy Ton, stationed at the entrance of the best runway shows, captures with great detail the style of fashion editors

for his Jak & Jil blog. Trends radiate both outside and on the runway, and his blog with pictures of studied style are a good example of this.

Suzy Menkes, fashion editor of the *International Herald Tribune* for the past twenty years, loved and feared in equal parts, has secured the front row at all worthwhile runways shows. The designer Alber Elbaz explains that the show does not begin until Menkes takes a seat, and Sophia Kokosalaki remembers the first time: "When she came to my show, I knew I was a designer."[7]

Menkes, who lives for "those moments when there is a sense that nothing after this show will ever be the same,"[8] it is common to see her totally absorbed in her work, sitting in the front row with her laptop on her legs waiting for the show to begin and taking notes during the show. Her reviews are important for the designers, who eagerly await her verdict. The night after his show, the designer at Lanvin Alber Elbaz has trouble falling asleep: ""When we designers do a good collection, Suzy is so happy for us, and when we do a bad one she seems almost to get angry."[9]

Sometimes, after a bad review, some designers, hurt by her comments, have vetoed her attendance for a few seasons. But time is a healer and one must take criticism with a pinch of salt and as a good sport. Miuccia Prada admitted in an interview that she paid attention to the reviews: "I don't believe that anyone is not bothered by criticism. I think that everybody cares," but points out: "There is a difference between caring and really being changed by it. I care because, of course, I'm a human being. That doesn't mean that I work for appreciation."[10]

It is important to separate the points of entry depending on the grouping of the guests, i.e. whether they are publishers, VIPs, press, buyers or general public. Once inside, the stewards and stewardesses, with help from the public relations team, will give exact instructions to the guests so they can find their seat easily. Name cards on each chair help facilitate this task. Public relations must have the complete list of guests as this will help with unexpected no-shows and to delay the runway show by a few minutes when waiting for the arrival of guests from other shows.

It is unusual for a show to start on time, but making the public wait excessively shows a lack of professionalism and preparation. Ten to fifteen minutes is the maximum allowed.

Let the show begin

The models lined up, one after the other, wait for their signal backstage to exit. Inside, the guests are seated and outside there is not a soul. Smooth communica-

RIGHT Hanne Gaby Odiele models in the spring-summer 2009 runway show by Dries van Noten. © Photography by Patrice Stable, courtesy of Dries van Noten. LEFT The same model waits impatiently in-line to walk out onto the runway. © Photography by Sonny Vandenvelde.

tion between the different areas is vital to determine when the show should begin. The lights are generally turned off and silence takes over the room.

The stage manager gives the nod and the first model appears. A monitor is installed backstage so that the designer, producer and team can follow the evolution of the runway show. The first model comes running and stands in front of the dresser, where, within minutes she is transformed into a new character in the collection. The makeup artist and hair stylist will take advantage of the time to touch up.

Outside, the public, in strict silence, which is only broken by claps of approval, has all eyes on the models and clothes, which move to the rhythm of the music and the flash of the photographers. The editors take note. One, three, twelve, eighteen, twenty-five and fifteen minutes later the last model appears backstage.

The music is turned off and now all the models, lined up or in group, go out to greet the audience. The designer also ventures out, with or without the models, walking the length of the runway or giving just a shy salute. Everything depends on the personality of the designer, although the public usually appreciates to be able to put a face to the creator of the pieces.

And then …

After so much effort, if the collection has gone down well, euphoria and exhaustion take over those present. The guests leave the room, the models remove their makeup, change and go to the next show, and part of the press demands, now more than ever, the designer's attention, who patiently responds to each of the questions while he/she is bombarded with impressions. One of the most interesting moments of the *Marc Jacobs & Louis Vuitton* documentary by Loïc Prigent is when, after the show, the designer, along with partner Robert Duffy, with barely enough strength to open his mouth, says: "I never believe what people tell me," and then a cut with a bunch of people congratulating Marc. In the car he continues to reflect: "When one finishes, the next one begins."

The evaluation

The day after, with the reviews in the daily press, an initial evaluation of the success of the runway show can be assessed. Those labels that fail to appear in the daily press will have to wait longer to see if it has succeeded in achieving media coverage in the specialized press. Now is a good time to self-criticize and evaluate what aspects have been mismanaged so as not to repeat the same mistakes in future events. Probing the team to identify problems is one of the best ways to gauge whether they have worked at ease, if there was carelessness and whether methodologies need to be improved.

Even in the runway shows with the biggest budgets, the most preparation and the best models, there is still room for contingencies and errors. But precisely this is the charisma of a presentation that takes six months to prepare and that only happens once.

Laird
Borre

Fashion editor
style.com

Laird Borrelli-Persson v
editor for *Style.com*, the
source of *Vogue* and *W* (C
From a young age she
fashion was her passion a
to take a Master's Degre
tory of fashion at the
stitute of Technology in
She combines her work
with a publishing editor, a
she has published *Fashi*
by Fashion Designers. Alo
Style.com team, Laird atte
shows in all the major fa
tals, a few weeks when sl
little sleep to be able t
events and review them v
four hours

In your opinion what is a runway show?

A runway show is a selection of outfits displayed by different models to a select audience. There are designers who have made history for how they have organized runway shows, such as Yves Saint Laurent, Hussein Chalayan, John Galliano for Christian Dior and Marc Jacobs.

What are the five key elements for a runway show to be a success?

All factors affect a runway show: teamwork, the models, art direction, etc. The combination of them all and a good team of professionals all contribute to success. But if I had to choose five key points are: the selection of garments that are going to be presented, the right number of looks, between twenty-four and thirty-six, the organization at the start of the runway show, a balanced pace in the presen-

tation of the clothes and, of course, the lighting.

What is your job as an editor for Style.com during fashion season?

Each season my colleagues and I try to attend all runway shows. I respect the creative process and try to be impartial setting aside my personal opinion about each designer. When assessing a runway show I consider whether or not the collection is in harmony with the context of the overall work of the designer, while also considering how the show fits in within the overall theme of the

runway show season. It is precisely this outfit that will set the trends which are then published in *Style.com*. Covering a fashion week online is like participating in a long-distance race, madness! Every day I attend five or eight runway shows and then I go to the office to write articles

and make the production for the next day. Thus, in *Style.com* you can find reviews and photos of the runway shows in only twenty-four hours. I spend the week trying to catch taxis and noting down model's names to not confuse any!

What are the invitations like to attend the runway shows from other designers?

There are many types of invitations to attend the runway shows. For a designer, the invitation is the presentation of the collection, a good invitation could be the deciding factor whether you attend a runway show or not. I have received invitations of all kinds: one in the shape of a scarf, another that was inside an old book by Virginia Woolf . . . I have a box full of invitations. Every season I keep those that I like the best. From my personal collection the one that stands out the most is the invitation that Rodarte sent out for his first runway shows, in envelopes decorated with old stamps.

Which designers currently put on the best runway shows?

During a runway show, a theatrical production can surprise

> ## "Covering a fashion week online is like participating in a long-distance race, madness"

me, as long as the garments are worth it. The runway shows are the best tool to show the looks that play with the silhouette. Some clothes can be better appreciated on the runway, especially if you sit close, as you notice all the details.

Why is the press release so important when preparing for a runway show?
A good press release gives the collection a context, it conveys the inspiration of the designer and creates an entire concept that later materializes in the runway show. It doesn't have to be a wordy text and should be no longer than one page. It must always include the contact information of the organizer as amidst the madness of fashion week you can never predict what could happen.

What criteria does Style.com *follow to select the designers who appear in the Fashion Shows column?*
We cover all the runway shows possible. Our main objective is to cover the luxury sector runway shows and then we try to add new collections and the newsworthy runway shows. We would cover many more, but we would need a larger team. We cover the runway shows of the fashion capitals (London, Paris, Milan and New York), and try to attend other cities, for example, I love the Copenhagen fashion week, which I usually go to but I do not always publish an article on it in *Style.com*.

Now that the online media publishes the photographs the day after the runway show, many people in the industry (including buyers) question the show as the cornerstone of the fashion system.
That's an ongoing debate to which no one has yet found an answer! It would benefit the environment that people and the clothes did not have to travel from one place to another, but it is very important to see the clothes and accessories before writing about them.

What advice would you give to emerging designers who are preparing their first runway show?
My advice would be that you do not have to put on a runway show to get a good name. Today there are many runway shows and they are so expensive to produce that I do not see the need. Editors are constantly attending runway shows and perhaps they are the best places so that emerging designers interact with us and can be seen. For me it's more important that young designers have a good catalogue of their collection ready to be delivered and a quality picture to be published, and then consider a runway show to exhibit their collection.

Clive Booth
www.clivebooth.co.uk

In the magical, sharp pictures by Clive Booth one can guess his pedigree. For over two decades he worked as a graphic designer and visual consultant for Adidas, Toyota and Moët & Chandon. A personal and polished look that can only be achieved with experience is present in each of the photographs of his recent splendid work as a photographer.

Daniel Mayer
www.danielmayer.com

With their pictures on the pages of the best magazines, whether it be *Vanity Fair*, *GQ* or *The New York Times*, Daniel approaches the world of fashion through images, and flees from the chaotic context associated with the backstage to create classical portraits full of content. Along with Christina Mayer, artistic director, they created *Backstage Magazine*.

David Ramos
www.davidramosphoto.com

Used to portraying the raw side of armed conflicts, the emotion in soccer fields and various social issues, in January 2008 he traveled to Paris on behalf of *Marie Claire* to show the haute couture fashion week from an unusual viewpoint. As a war photographer, David has dissected and caught on camera what has most caught his attention.

Eric Oliveira
www.flickr.com/photos/ericska

Of Brazilian origin and currently residing in London, Eric is a versatile photographer with interests in many areas, art, music or fashion, and it shows in his way of approaching the models in the different backstage sets from Milan to Paris. When they pose, he manages to create a special bond, where sensuality and elegance are ever-present.

Eyesight
www.eyesight.fr

Founded in 2002, this agency designs and produces runway shows for Dior Homme, Sophia Kokosalaki, Giambattista Valli and Kris van Assche. To organize events of this magnitude, his team includes the experienced talent of Thierry Dreyfus as artistic director and Marie Meresse as production director.

Gerard Estadella
www.icanteachyouhowtodoit.com

Gerard shoots mostly at night, usually in the best parties full of celebrities when they really get into swing. Besides covering, in detail, the afterparties for Galliano, Balenciaga and Jeremy Scott, he still has the strength to attend runway shows and show us what goes on, whether backstage, front row, or on the runway.

Gi Myao
www.gimyao.com

Divine, impressionist and humorous, the drawings of the fashion illustrator Gi Myao convey both aesthetics and character. His personal style has captivated brands like Zara, Harvey Nichols or LFW Daily Rubbish. For someone who started to sketch with Chanel red lipstick, a less glamorous future could not be envisaged.

Jarno Ketunen
www.jarnok.com

His backstage drawings are the result of the immediacy of the moment. Taken live at the curtains of the Dior Homme, Jean Paul Gaultier or Bruno Pieters shows, they are imbued with the emotion of the moment. Sketches done in minutes, with his gestural strokes, he offers a different alternative and personal registry to that of photography.

Mark Reay
www.backstagesideshow.com

When not taking pictures in the sets of Hollywood blockbusters, Mark Reay uses the magazine *Dazed & Confused* to access the busiest backstage settings during New York Fashion Week to show the close-up beauty of the slender models as well as the entire team.

OMA
www.oma.eu

The collaboration between architect Rem Koolhass and Prada began in 2001 with the design of the Italian firm's main store in Manhattan. This project was the first of a rich and prolific collaboration, which has also led to the design the Prada runways, where Koolhaas' intellectual stamp does not go unnoticed.

Sonny Vandevelde
www.sonnyphotos.typepad.com

Restless and vivacious, Sonny travels the world to attend from the backstage all those runway shows he is invited to, whether it is an exclusive launch event in Paris or an independent show in Athens. His passion for fashion and his friendships with models, designers and journalists makes his pictures full of complicity and authenticity.

Villa Eugénie
www.villaeugenie.com

Étienne Russo and his team are responsible for the majestic and theatrical Chanel runway shows, the aesthetic and artistic set designs by Dries van Noten and the groundbreaking and nonconforming presentations of Maison Martin Margiela. For each designer, a style with a common denominator: to leave all present with their mouths wide open.

Find out more

DazedDigital
dazeddigital.com

DeMode
www.demode.se

Dirrty Glam
dirrtyglam.com

Fashion.net
www.fashion.net

Fashionologie
www.fashionologie.com

Hintmag
www2.hintmag.com

Interview Magazine
www.interviewmagazine.com

"IT
www.itfashion.com

Nylon Magazine
www.nylonmag.com

PonyStep Magazine
www.ponystep.com

Refinery29
www.refinery29.com

Showstudio
www.showstudio.com

Style
www.style.com

Stylelist
www.stylelist.com

The Love Magazine
www.thelovemagazine.co.uk

Vogue
www.style.com/vogue

Wallpaper
www.wallpaper.com/fashion

Zoo Magazine
www.zoomagazine.de

Fashion in images

160g
www.160grams.com

Acne Paper
www.acnestudios.com/acne-paper

Amelia's Magazine
www.ameliasmagazine.com

Backstage Magazine
www.backstage-mag.com

Crash
www.crash.fr

Dresslab
www.dresslab.com

Fantastic Man
www.fantasticman.com

Fashion156
www.fashion156.com

Flaunt Magazine
flaunt.com

Fly 16x9 Magazine
fly16x9.com

Iconique
www.iconique.com

i-D Magazine
www.i-dmagazine.com/primary_index.htm

Lula Magazine
www.lulamag.com

Metal Magazine
revistametal.com

NEO2
www.neo2.es

Pop Magazine
thepop.com

Purple Magazine
www.purple.fr

Russh Magazine
russhmagazine.com/russh/home.html

Sesame Media
www.sesamemedia.com

Tush Magazine
www.tushmagazine.com

Zoozoom
www.zoozoom.com

Feed your curiosity with the latest

Business of Fashion
www.businessoffashion.com

Fashion Week Daily
fashionweekdaily.com

Fashion Wire Daily
www.fashionwiredaily.com

International Herald Tribune
www.nytimes.com/pages/fashion

JC Report
www.jcreport.com

Modem Online
www.modemonline.com

The Fashion Spot
www.thefashionspot.com

The Moment
themoment.blogs.nytimes.com

Unit-f
www.unit-f.at

wwd
www.wwd.com

Blogs

A Shaded View on Fashion
www.ashadedviewonfashion.com

Blog Couture
http://blogcouture.info

Bored&Beautiful
http://blog.styleserver.de

Coute que Coute
www.coutequecoute.de

Fart Guide
http://fartguide.blogspot.com

Fashion Projects
fashionprojects.org

Fashion Reality
www.fashionreality.blogspot.com

Fashionista
www.fashionista.com

Fifi Lapin
www.fifi-lapin.blogspot.com

Is Mental
is-mental.blogspot.com

Jak & Jil
jakandjil.blogspot.com

Jargol
www.jargol.com

Kate Loves Me
www.katelovesme.net

Kingdom of Style
kingdomofstyle.typepad.co.uk

Miss at la Playa
missatlaplaya.blogspot.com

Notcouture
www.notcouture.com

Style Bubble
stylebubble.typepad.com

Tavi
tavi-thenewgirlintown.blogspot.com

The Clones
theclones.eu

The Coveted
the-coveted.com/blog

The Fashion Observer
www.thefashionobserver.com

The Imagist
theimagist.com

Model agencies

Confessions of a Casting Director
coacdinc.com

DNA Models
www.dnamodels.com/news-letter

Elite London
elitelondon.blogspot.com

Models.com
models.com

One Management News
onemanagement.com/news

Supreme Management
www.suprememanagement.com/being

Uno Bcn
www.unobcn.com

Women Management Blog
womenmanagement.blogspot.com

Women Paris Management
womenmanagementparis.blogspot.com

Production agencies

Atelier Lum
www.atelierlum.com

Bureau Betak
www.bureaubetak.com

Eyesight
www.eyesight.fr

Gainsbury and Whiting
www.gainsburyandwhiting.com/

La Mode en Images
www.mode-images.com

LOT experimental spaces
lot71.com

Obo Global
www.oboglobal.com

Spec Entertainment
www.specentertainment.com

Thierry Dreyfus
www.thierry-dreyfus.com

Villa Eugénie
www.villaeugenie.com

Creative agencies

Almudena Madera
almudenamadera.com

Art+Commerce
www.artandcommerce.com/aac/startpage.aspx

Blow
www.blow.co.uk

Clm
www.clmus.com

Hunter&Gatti
http://hunterandgatti.blogspot.com

Jed Root
www.jedroot.com

Kaastel Agent
www.kasteelagent.com

MAP LTD
www.mapltd.com

Motif Management
www.motifmanagement.com

Poetic Artists
www.poeticartists.com

Streeters London
www.streeterslondon.com

Public relations and press

Fashion Press Release
www.fashionpressrelease.com

Mao
www.maopr.com

People's Revolution
www.peoplesrevolution.com

Pressing Online
www.pressingonline.com

Relative
www.relative-london.com

Système D
www.systeme-d.net

Photography

Catwalking
www.catwalking.com

Go Backstage
gobackstage.blogspot.com

Marcio Madeira
www.firstview.com

Mark Reay
www.markreay.net

Sonny Photos
www.sonnyphotos.typepad.com

Fashion Weeks

9Festival for Fashion & Photography
www.9festival.at

Australian Fashion Week
rafw.com.au

Barcelona Fashion Week
www.080barcelonafashion.com

Berlin Fashion Week
www.mercedes-benzfashionweek.com

Copenhagen Fashion Week
www.copenhagenfashionweek.com

Japan Fashion Week
www.jfw.jp/

London Fashion Week
www.londonfashionweek.co.uk

Madrid Fashion Week
www.ifema.es/ferias/cibeles

Milan Fashion Week
www.cameramoda.it

New York Fashion Week
www.mbfashionweek.com

Paris Fashion Week
www.modeaparis.com

São Paulo Fashion Week
www.spfw.com.br/

Vienna Fashion Week
www.mqviennafashionweek.com/

Villa Noailles
www.villanoailles-hyeres.com/

Bibliography

Monographs

Bernard, Malcolm: *Fashion as Communication*. Routledge, 2002.

Breward, Christopher and David Gilbert: *Fashion's World Cities*. Cultures of Consumption Series. Berg Publishers, 2006.

Bruzzi, Stella and Pamela Church Gibson: *Fashion Cultures: Theories, Explorations and Analysis*. Routledge, 2001.

Evans, Caroline: *Fashion at the Edge: Spectacle, Modernity and Deathliness*. Yale University Press, 2003.

Figueras, Josefina: *Protagonistas de la moda*. Ediciones Internacionales Universitarias.

Gehlhar, Mary: *The Fashion Designer Survival Guide: An Insider's Look at Starting and Running Your Own Fashion Business*. Kaplan Business, 2005.

Goworek, Helen: *Fashion Buying*. Wiley Blackwell, 2001.

Jackson, Tim and David Shaw: *The Fashion Handbook*. Routledge, 2006.

Jenkyn Jones, Sue: *Fashion Design*. Watson-Guptill, 2002.

Martínez Caballero, Elsa and Ana Isabel Vázquez Casco: *Márqueting de la moda*. Ediciones Pirámide, 2006.

Del Olmo Arriaga, José Luis: *Marketing de la moda*. Ediciones Internacionales Universitarias.

Pochna, Marie-France: ffcfflDior. Universo de la Modaff/cffl. Ediciones Polígrafa, 1997.

Quick, Harriet: *Catwalking: A History of the Fashion Model*. Booksales, 1999.

Quinn, Bradley: *Techno Fashion*. Berg Publishers, 2002.

Schweitzer, Marlis: *When Broadway Was the Runway: Theater, Fashion and American Culture*. University of Pennsylvania Press, 2008.

Sorber, Richard and Jenny Udale: *Principios básicos del diseño de moda*. Gustavo Gili, 2008.

Tungate, Mark: *Marcas de moda. Marcar estilo desde Armani a Zara*. Gustavo Gili, 2008.

White, Nicola and Ian Griffiths: *The Fashion Business: Theory, Practice, Image. Dress, Body*. Culture Series. Berg Publishers, 2000.

Wilcox, Claire: *Radical Fashion*. Victoria and Albert Museum Studies, 2001.

Williams, Roshumba: *The Complete Idiot's Guide to Being a Model*. Alpha, 1999.

Zazzo, Anne, et. al.: *Fashion show. Les desfilades de moda*. Museu Tèxtil i d'Indumentaria

Magazines

Baldenweg, Nora: "Wonder Woman," *Russh Magazine*, July-August 2009.

Callender, Cat: "Fashion & style: the model maker," *The Independent*, 29 September 2005.

Cocgard, Catherine: "Alexandre de Betak, scénographe de mode," *Le Temps*, 24 September 2008.

Ellis, D.: "Show," *Big Magazine*, 2006, nº 63.

Orecklin, Michele: "The Shape of Things to Come: Pat McGrath," *Time Style & Design*, Spring 2003.

Prigent, Loïc: "Alex de Betak, Le Cecil B. De Mille des podiums," *Mixt(e) Magazine*, March-April 2004.

Rousseau, Carole: "Les Producteurs," *Le Figaro*, 27 February 2007.

Online articles

Barber, Lynn: "Why Katie Grand is the most-wanted woman in fashion," *Guardian.co.uk*, http://www.guardian.co.uk/lifeandstyle/2008/jul/06/women.fashion2 [see: 06/07/2008].

Blakeley, Kiri: "How To Be A Supermodel," *Forbes.com*, http://www.forbes.com/2007/10/02/modeling-moss-bundchen-biz-media_cz_kb_1003supermodels.html [see: 10/03/2007].

Borrelli-Persson, Laird: "Rodarte Fashion Show Review," *Style.com*,http://www.style.com/fashionshows/review/F2009RTW-RODARTE [see: 17/02/2009].

Breslin, Yale: "Meet Greg Kessler," *StarWorks Blog*, http://starworksny.com/blog/2009/01/20/meet-greg-kessler [see: 20/01/2009].

Bumpus, Jessica: "Jensen's LFW Move", *Vogue.com*, http://www.vogue.co.uk/news/daily/090813-peter-jensen-to-do-a-presentation-i.aspx [see: 13/08/2009].

Carter, Lee: "Hedi Slimane: Dior's Homme Away from Home," *Hint Fashion Magazine*, http://www.hintmag.com/hinterview/hedislimane/hedislimane1.php [see: 19/11/2009].

Cartner-Morley, Jess: "Modesty Blaze," *Guardian.co.uk*, http://www.guardian.co.uk/lifeandstyle/2005/feb/26/shopping.fashion1#history-byline [see: 26/02/2005].

Doig, Stephen: "Christopher Kane: Show Report," *Vogue UK*, http://www.vogue.co.uk/fashion/show.aspx/catwalk-report/id,3882 [see: 20/10/2006].

Foley, Bridget: "Smart Sex," *W Magazine*, http://www.wmagazine.com/fashion/2009/09/prada [see: 19/09/2009].

Fortini, Amanda: "How the Runway Took Off," *Slate Magazine*, http://www.slate.com/id/2173464/ [see: 06/09/2007].

Graham, David: "Alexander McQueen brings once-exclusive show online," *TheStar.com*, http://www.thestar.com/living/fashion/article/705809--alexander-mcqueen-brings-once-exclusive-show-online [see: 06/10/2007].

Griffiths, Liz: "Christopher Kane: New Gen Profile," *Female First*, http://www.femalefirst.co.uk/lifestyle-fashion/styletrendsChristopher+Kane+New+Gen+Profile-4373.html [see: 21/01/2008].

Healy, Murray: "Katie Grand: She's Popping Out," *Hint Fashion Magazine*, http://www.hintmag.com/hinterview/katiegrand/katiegrand2.php [see: 19/11/2009].

Kowalewski, Katharina: "Carine Roitfeld Interview, Marc by Marc Jacobs Show, NYC," *KO. Fashion*, http://blog.kofashion.com/post/2008/04/19/CARINE-ROITFELD-INTERVIEW [see: 19/04/2008].

Kowalewski, Katharina: "Bernhard Willhelm Interview," *KO Fashion*, http://blog.kofashion.com/post/2008/04/2/CARINE-ROITFELD-INTERVIEW [see: 02/10/2008].

Landman, Kyle: "Welcome to the Dollhouse," *JC Report*, http://www.jcreport.com/interviews/180608/welcome-dollhouse [see: 18/06/2008].